Short 'a' as in 'cat'

Find the correct word. Ring it.

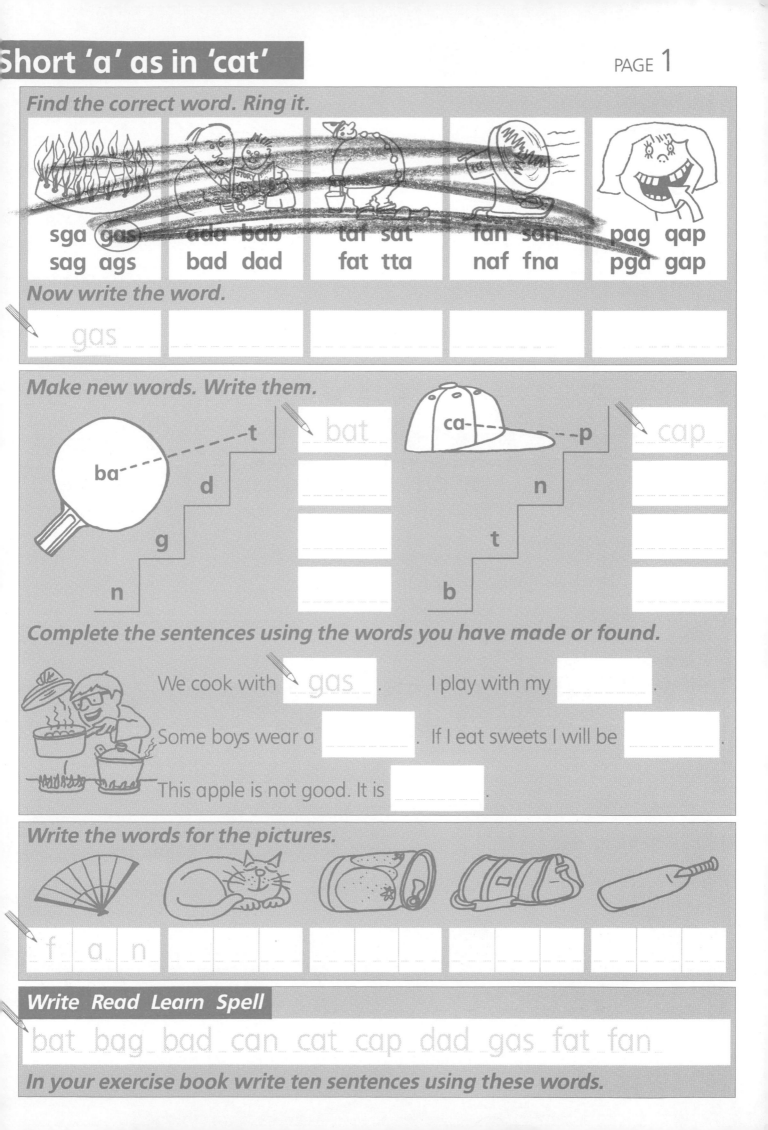

| sga **gas** | ada bab | taf sat | fan san | pag qap |
| sag ags | bad dad | fat tta | naf fna | pga gap |

Now write the word.

gas | | | |

Make new words. Write them.

ba — t   bat   ca- - - -p   cap

d

g

n

n

t

b

Complete the sentences using the words you have made or found.

We cook with __gas__ .   I play with my _____ .

Some boys wear a _____ .   If I eat sweets I will be _____ .

This apple is not good. It is _____ .

Write the words for the pictures.

f a n | | | |

In your exercise book write ten sentences using these words.

Make new words. Write them.

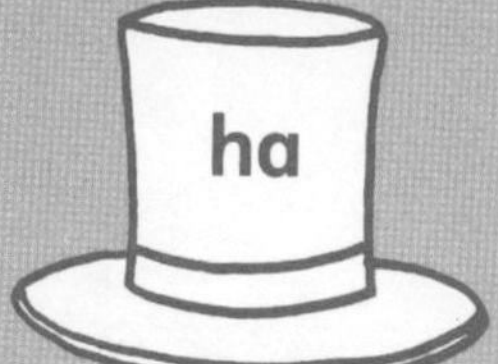

ha — t, d, m → hat

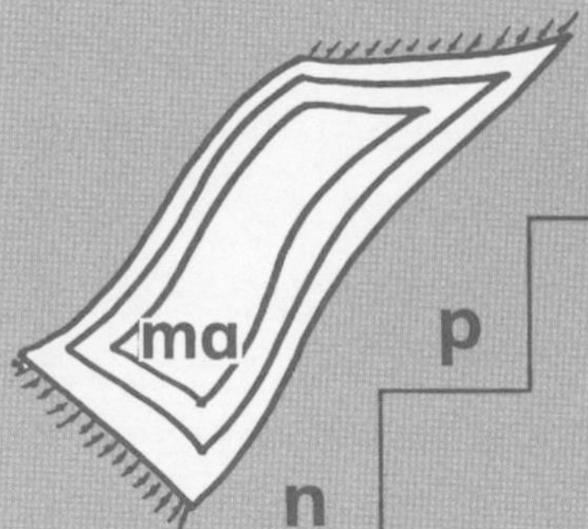

ma — t, p, n, d

Find the correct word. Ring it.

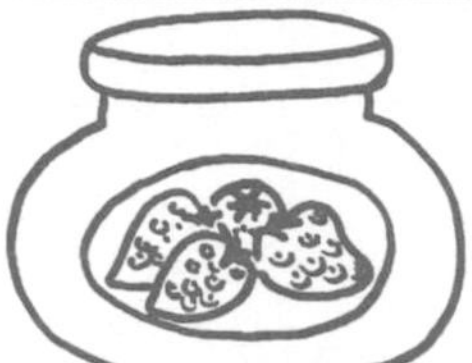

jan (jam) maj jem

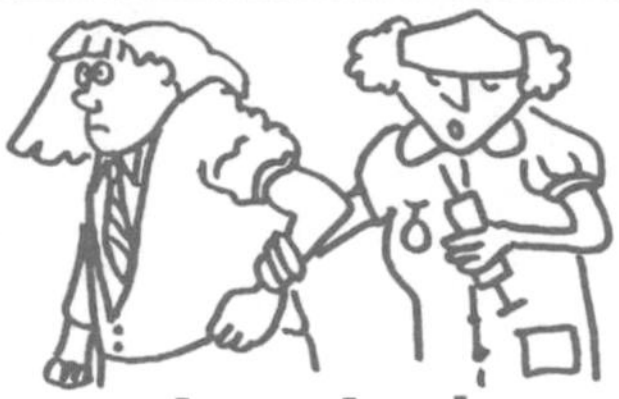

jat jad jap jab

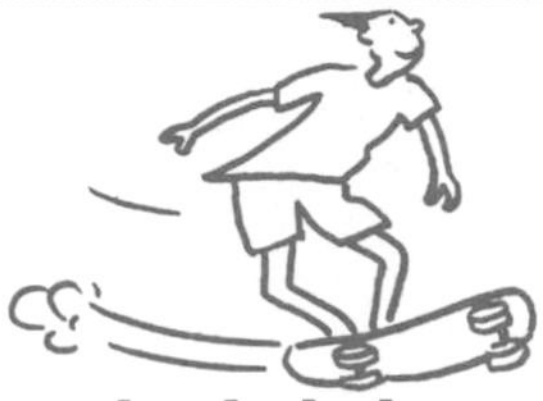

lad lab lap lba

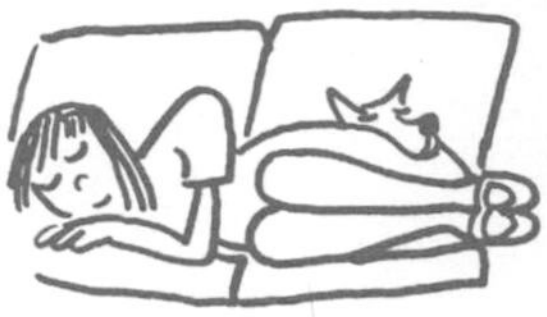

naq nap nab nad

Now write the word.

jam

Write the words for the pictures.

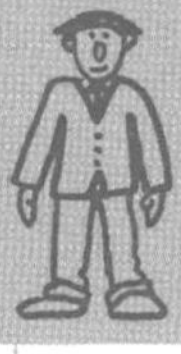

m a n

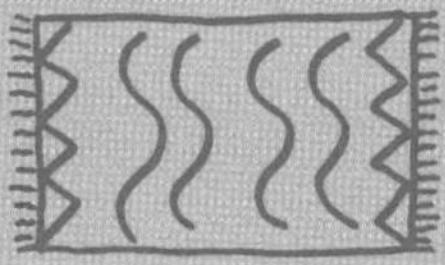

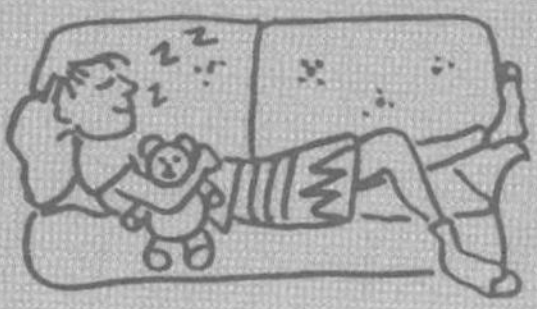

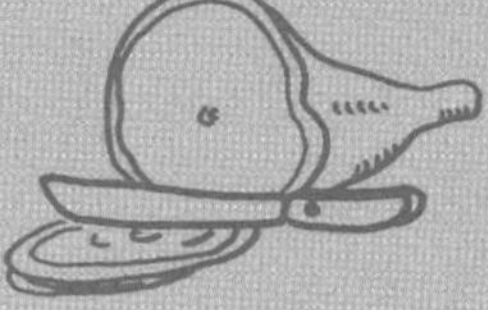

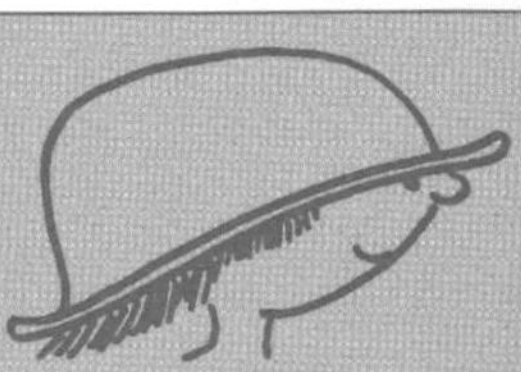

Complete the sentences using the words you have made.

We __had__ fish for tea.   Something we wear on our heads. →

We had _____ sandwiches for tea.   The cat sat on the _____.

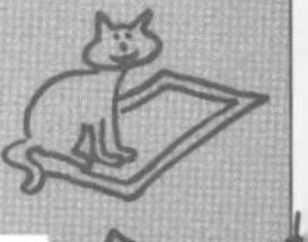

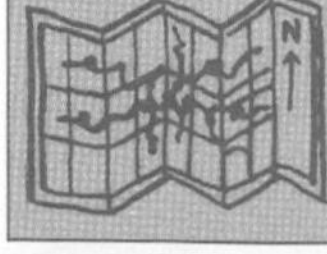

A _____ tells you the way.   The nurse gave me a _____.

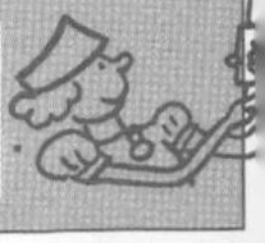

In your exercise book write ten sentences using these words.

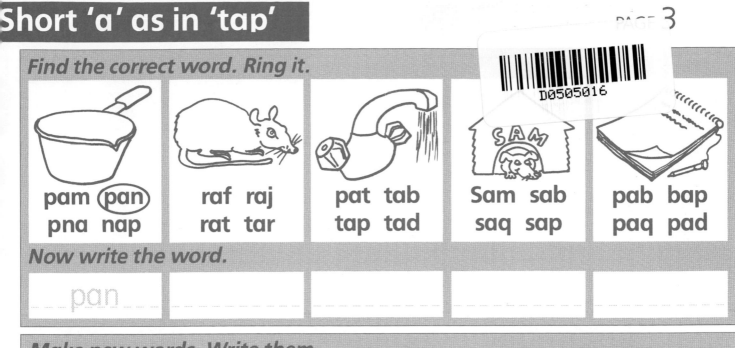

Find the correct word. Ring it.

| pam (pan) pna nap | raf raj rat tar | pat tab tap tad | Sam sab saq sap | pab bap paq pad |

Now write the word.

| pan | | | | |

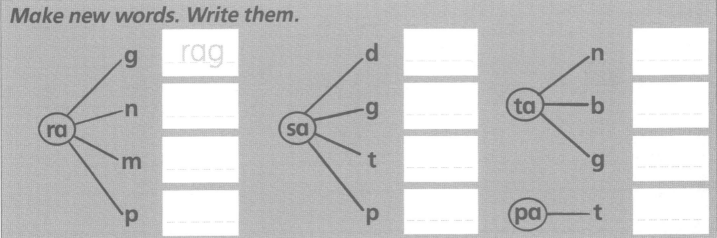

Make new words. Write them.

ra — g / n / m / p   rag

sa — d / g / t / p

ta — n / b / g
pa — t

Write the words for the pictures.

r a m

Complete the sentences using the words you have made.

A male sheep is a ___ram___   My dog is called S_____

He _____ away.   A man _____ on a chair.

Something we cook in. → _____

sat sad tap pat pad pan rag rat ram ran

In your exercise book write ten sentences using these words.

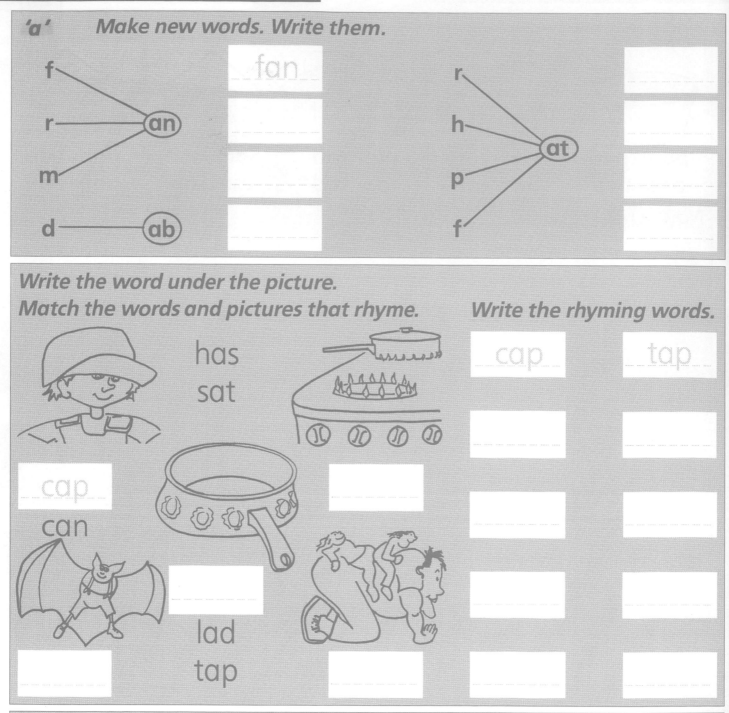

'a' *Make new words. Write them.*

f —
r — (an)
m —
d — (ab)

fan

r —
h — (at)
p —
f —

Write the word under the picture.
Match the words and pictures that rhyme.   *Write the rhyming words.*

has
sat

cap

can

lad
tap

cap   tap

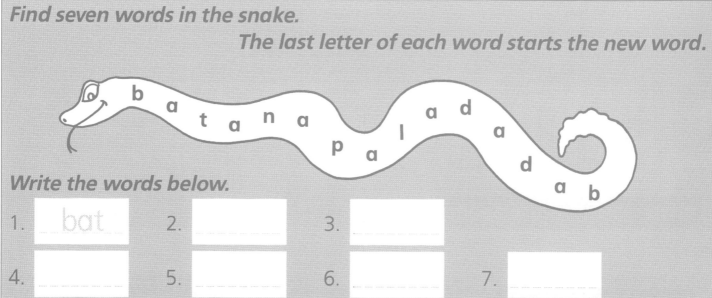

Find seven words in the snake.
The last letter of each word starts the new word.

b a t a n a p a l a d a d a b

Write the words below.

1. bat   2.   3.

4.   5.   6.   7.

Make new words. Write them.

a — s → as
a — t →
a — n →
a — m →

h — e →
m — e →
b — e →
w — e →

i — n →
i — s →
i — f →
i — t →

o — h →
o — f →
o — n →
o — ff →
o — r →

u — p →
u — s →

Complete the sentences using the words you have made.

The cat is __in__ the window.

__W__ play in the garden.

Paul is climbing _____ the ladder.

__I__ it rains we will get wet.

We will need _____ umbrella.

Find the hidden words. Write them.

plant — _an_

Jon — _____

basket — _____

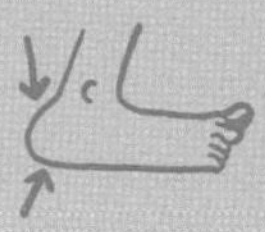

heel — _____

fifty — _____

toffee — _____

in is it of on up at we off he

In your exercise book write ten sentences using these words.

Short 'e' as in 'bed'

Add 'e' to make a word.

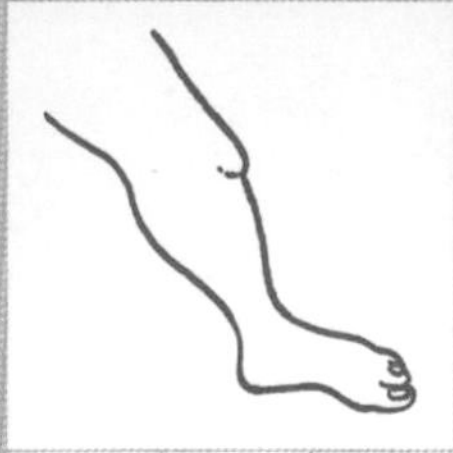

l e g

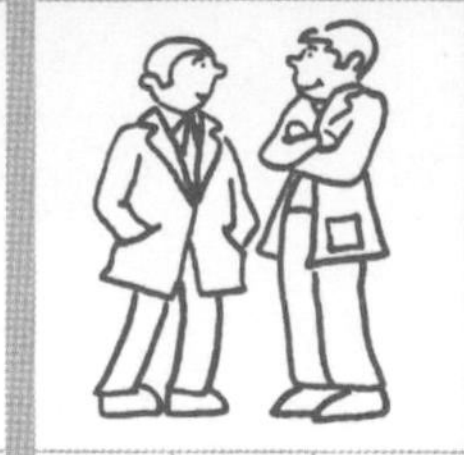

m _ n

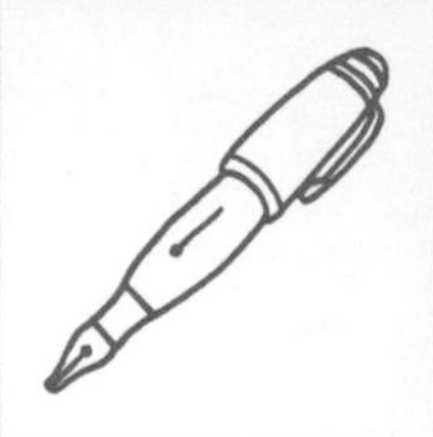

p _ n

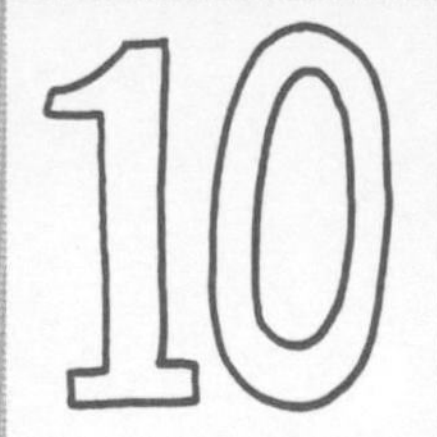

t _ n

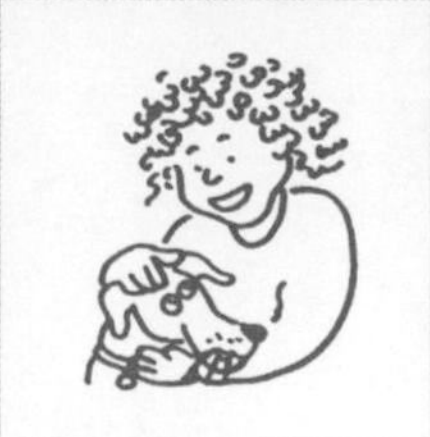

p _ t

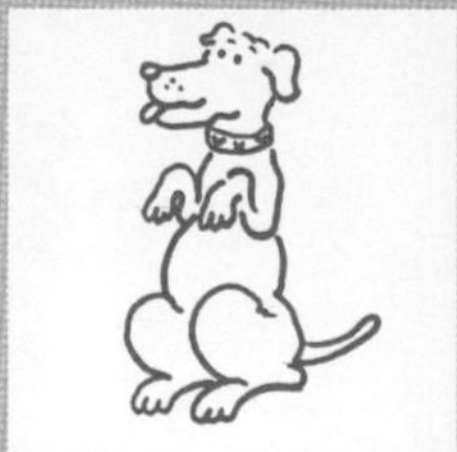

b _ g

Now write the word.

Find the correct word. Ring it.

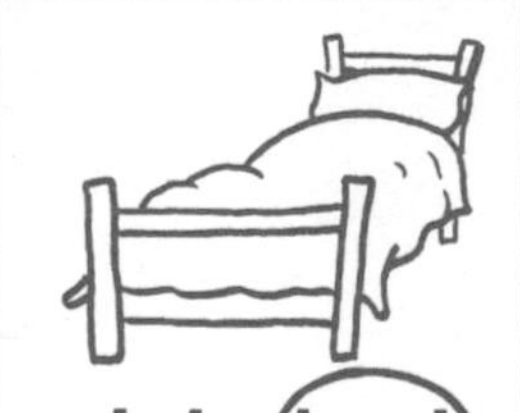

deb (bed) ded beb

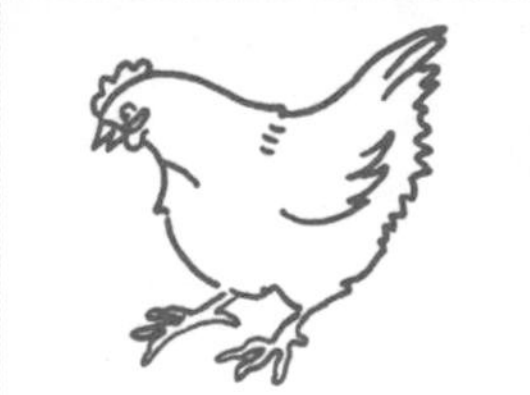

hen hem meh ehm

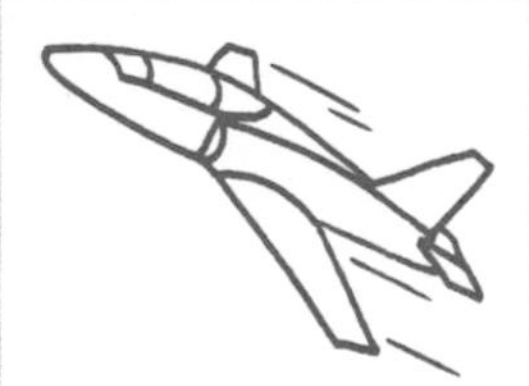

jat tej jet jek

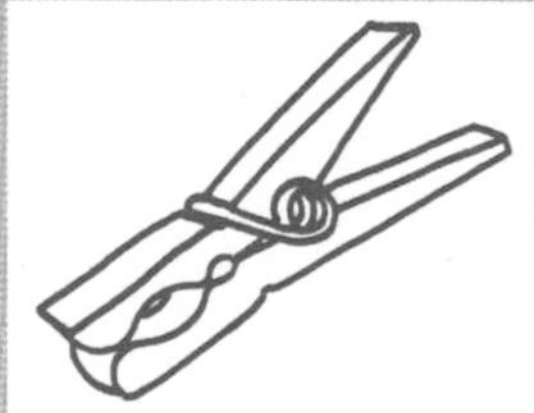

qeg gep pge peg

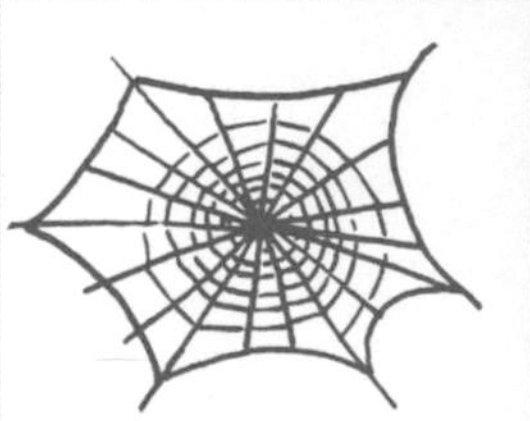

bew dew web wed

Now write the word.

bed

Make new words. Write them.

re, le, fe → d

we, ge → t

le, me → t

Complete the words in the puzzle.

I sleep in my _ e _.

A colour. → _ e _

Not dry. → _ e _

A spider makes a _ e _.

Write Read Learn Spell

leg bed get men met pet pen ten wet let

In your exercise book write ten sentences using these words.

Find the correct word. Ring it.

did dip bid (bib)	fib fid fig fgi	kib kid dik kip	fif fit tif fil	fin nif fim fiu

Now write the word.

bib

Make new words. Write them.

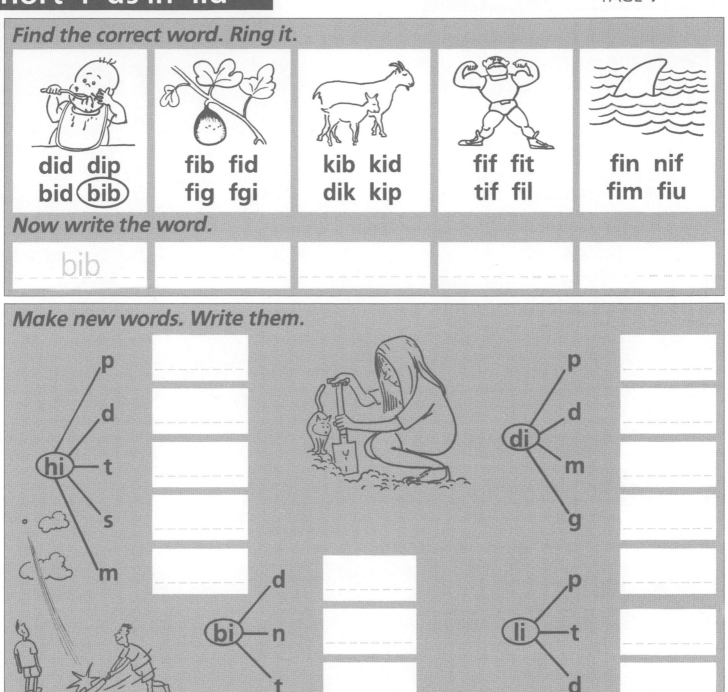

hi — p, d, t, s, m

di — p, d, m, g

bi — d, n, t

li — p, t, d

Complete the sentences using the words you have made.

I _____ with my spade.

The light is _____ .

The boy _____ the ball.

I _____ the toy in the box.

I saw _____ and he saw me.

Emma _____ her homework.

Write Read Learn Spell

bit bin did fin fit dig hid him his hit

In your exercise book write ten sentences using these words.

Add a letter to make a word.
Write the word.

pi — g
pi — n
pi — t

ri — b
ri — d
ri — m
ri — p

t
w   in
b

s
t   ip
h

p
s   it
w

Write 'i' to make a new word.

w	i	g
n		b
r		p
p		p

Now write the word.

wig

Complete the sentences using the words you have made.

My pen has a ....   A farm animal. →

We play in the sand ....   The biscuits are in the ....

I run in a race to ....   The judge wears a ....

You may have a .... of my milk

Write Read Learn Spell

pig pin pit rib rip pip tin tip win rid

In your exercise book write ten sentences using these words.

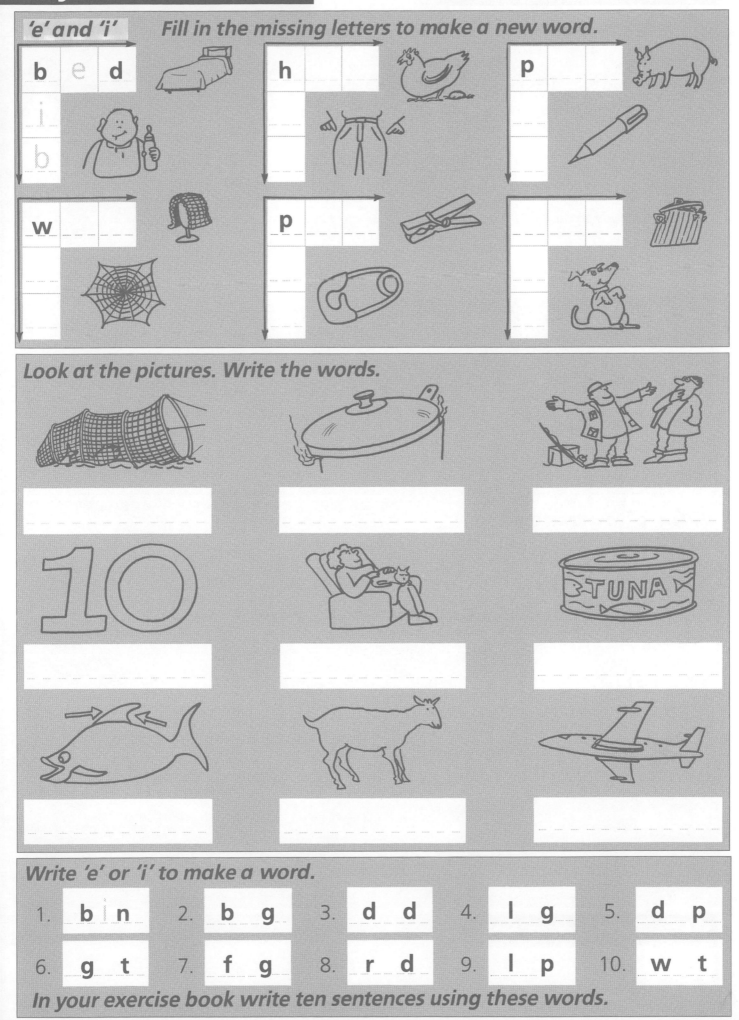

'e' and 'i' *Fill in the missing letters to make a new word.*

b	e	d
i		
b		

h	

p		

w		

p		

Look at the pictures. Write the words.

Write 'e' or 'i' to make a word.

1. **b** i **n**   2. **b** __ **g**   3. **d** __ **d**   4. **l** __ **g**   5. **d** __ **p**

6. **g** __ **t**   7. **f** __ **g**   8. **r** __ **d**   9. **l** __ **p**   10. **w** __ **t**

In your exercise book write ten sentences using these words.

Short 'o' as in 'dog'

Find the correct word. Ring it.

| cob cod | cof cto | ogc cgo | god dog | bot tob |
| cdo doc | toc cot | cog goc | gdo bog | otd dot |

Now write the word.

Make new words. Write them.

jo — b
jo — g
jo — t

ho — t
ho — b
ho — p

Fill in 'o' to make a word.

c__b   g__t   p__d

Complete the sentences using the words you have made.

My ___dog___ is called Spot.   Dad likes to _____ .

The water is _____ .   I _____ down my notes.

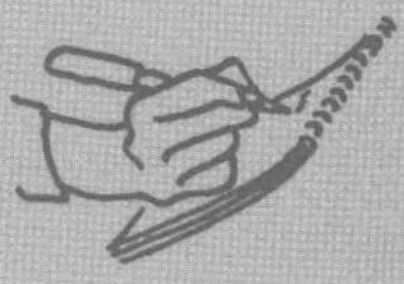

I can _____ .   The wheel has a missing _____ .

Write Read Learn Spell

hob cot dog hop hot jot got dot jog job

In your exercise book write ten sentences using these words.

Find the correct word. Ring it.

nop wop
mpo mop

rob bor
rod rop

tod top
toq tob

sob sop
osd sap

Now write the word.

Join 3 letters to make a word. Write the words.

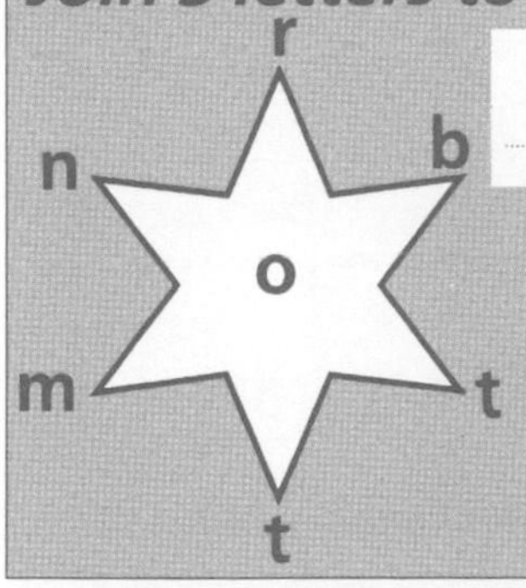

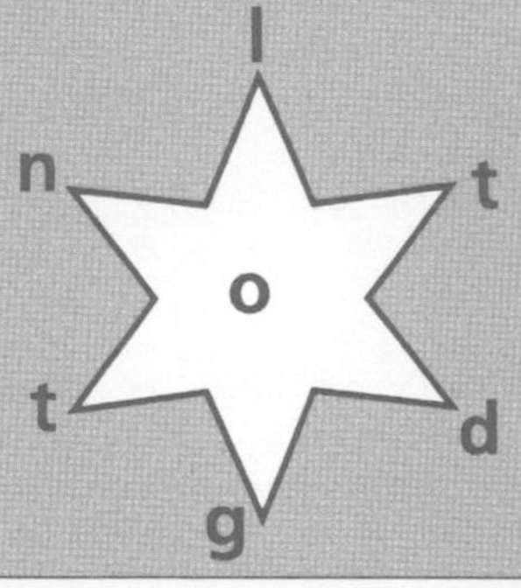

r
n   b
   o
m   t
   t

l
n   t
   o
t   d
   g

Complete the words in the puzzle.

Do . . . touch!

Crowd of people. → . . .

To cry. → . . .

I have a . . . of friends.

I fish with my . . . .

Part of a tree. → . . .

I can . . . my head to say yes.

Write Read Learn Spell

log lot mop nod not top sob rob rod rot

In your exercise book write ten sentences using these words.

Write 'u' in the middle to make a word.

| j | u | g |  | m | | g | | | n | | t |  | p | | | p |  | r | | | g |  | s | | n |

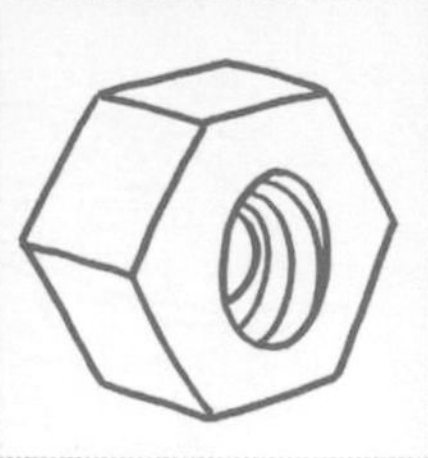

Now write the word.

Join 3 letters to make a word. Write the words.

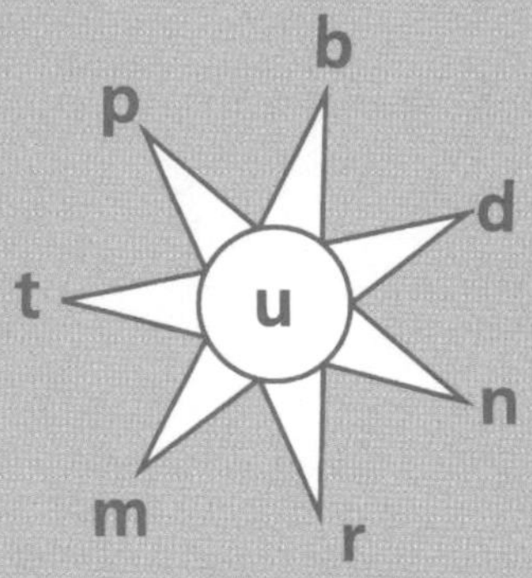

p
b
t — u — d
m — r — n

pub

s — p — b
t — u — g
r — t — m

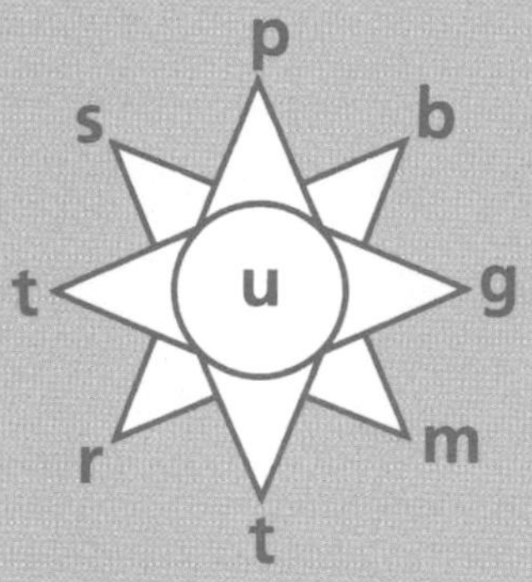

Complete the words in the puzzle.

Adults can buy drinks at the . . .   _ u _

5 + 5 is a . . .   _ u _

. . . on your coat.   _ u _

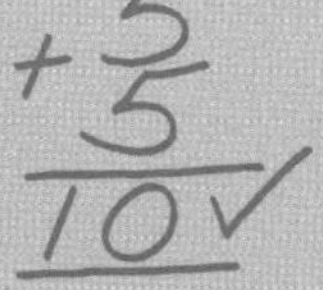

I can . . . very fast. $+\dfrac{5}{5}$ $\overline{10}$ ✓   _ u _

The cat sat on the . . .   _ u _

Rub a dub dub three men in a . . .   _ u _

In your exercise book write ten sentences using these words.

Make new words. Write them.

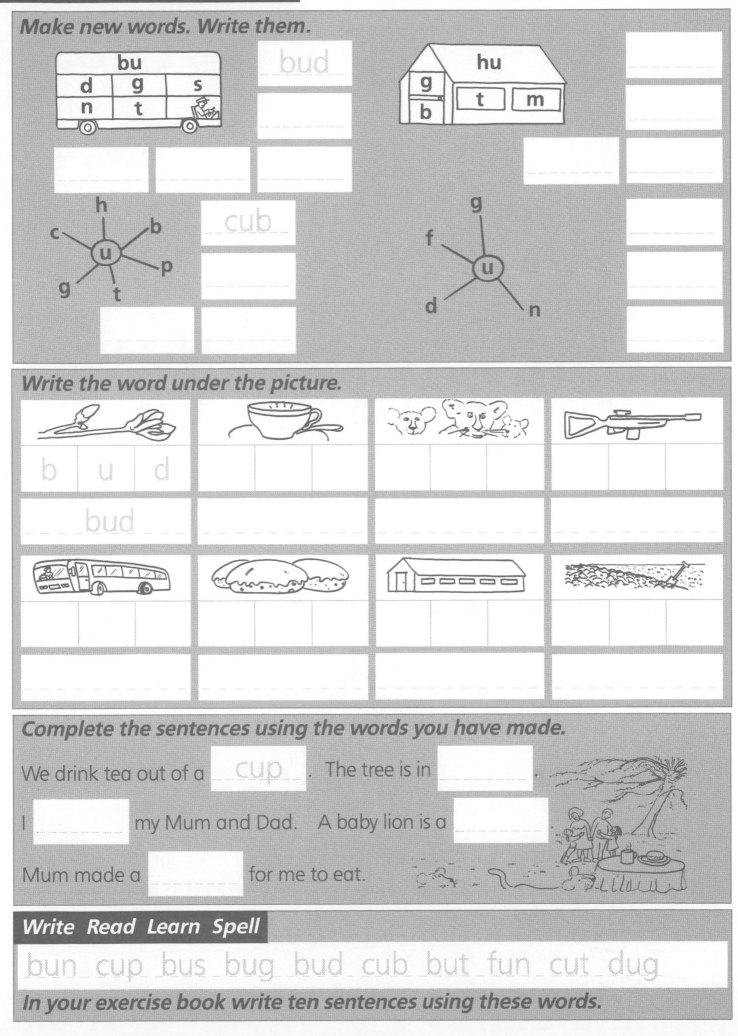

Write the word under the picture.

b u d

bud

Complete the sentences using the words you have made.

We drink tea out of a _cup_ . The tree is in _____ .

I _____ my Mum and Dad.   A baby lion is a _____ .

Mum made a _____ for me to eat.

'o' and 'u' — *Look at the pictures. Write the words.*

bud

Add 'o' or 'u' to make a word. Complete the word.

b o g	p t	g t	d g	h p
l t	f n	t p	h t	s b

Complete the words in the puzzle.

1. Three men in a . . .
2.
3.
4. wet soil
5.
6.
7.

t u b

8.
9.
10.
11. a tiny insect
12. Have you . . . a pet?
13.
14. a pea . . .

Can you remember?

a e i o u   **Write twelve words in the snake.
The last letter of each word starts the next word.**

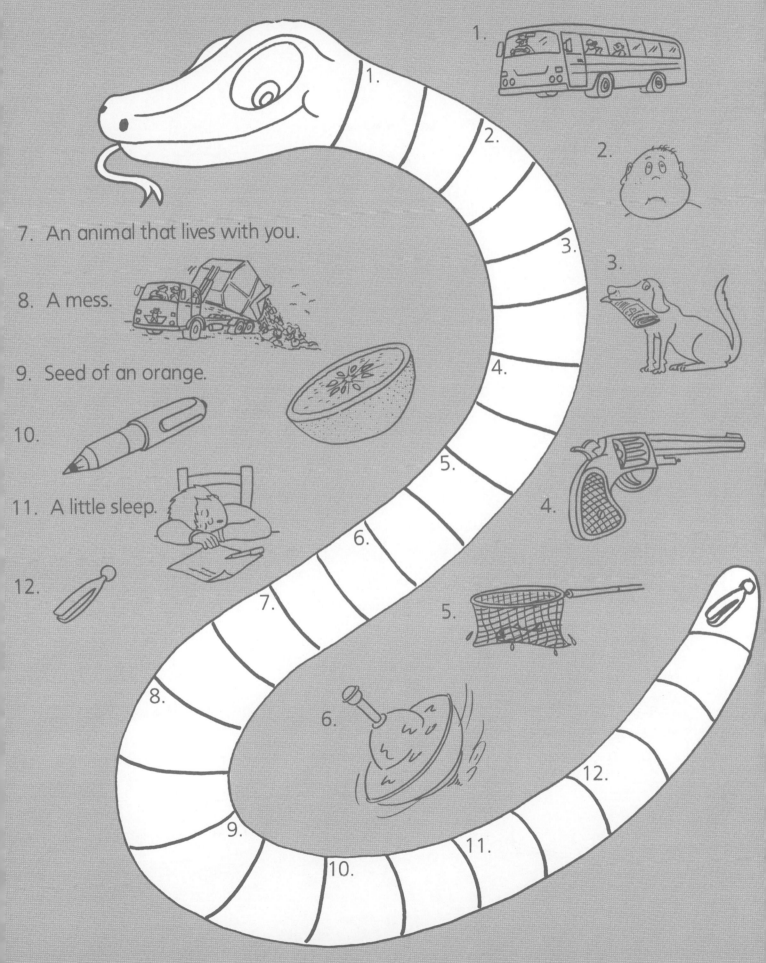

7. An animal that lives with you.

8. A mess.

9. Seed of an orange.

10.

11. A little sleep.

12.

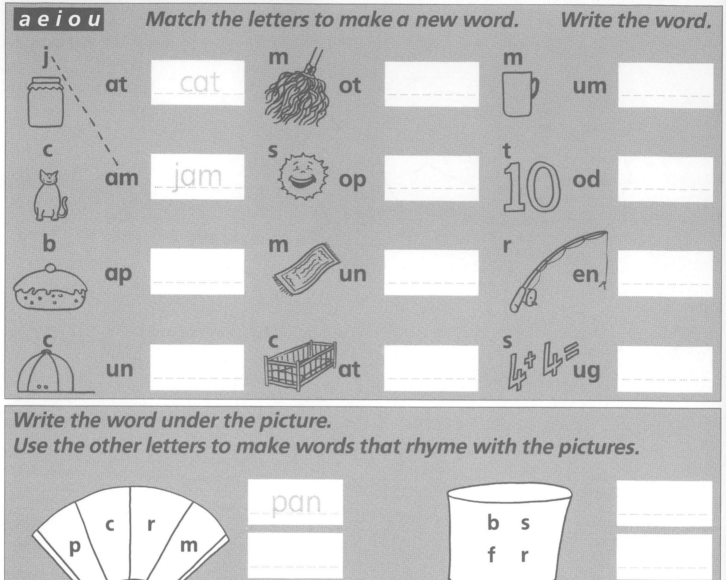

a e i o u *Match the letters to make a new word.* *Write the word.*

j — at   cat
m — ot
m — um

c — am   jam
s — op
t — od

b — ap
m — un
r — en

c — un
c — at
s — ug

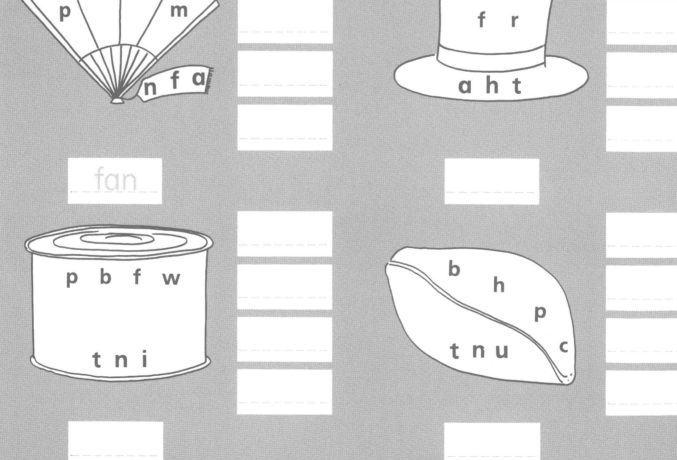

Write the word under the picture.
Use the other letters to make words that rhyme with the pictures.

pan

fan

Make new words to rhyme with this first word.

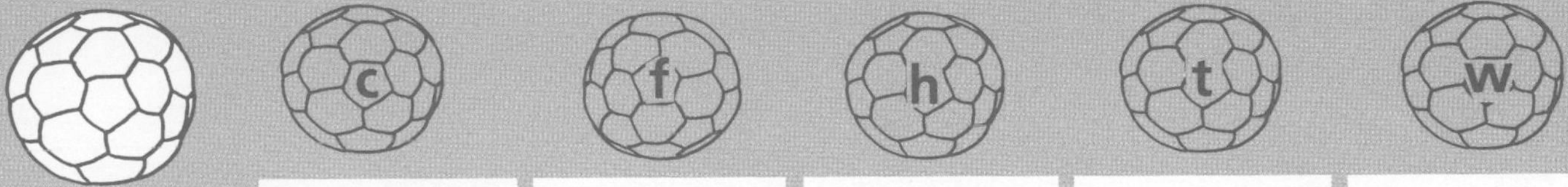

ball	**c** call	**f**	**h**	**t**	**w**

bell	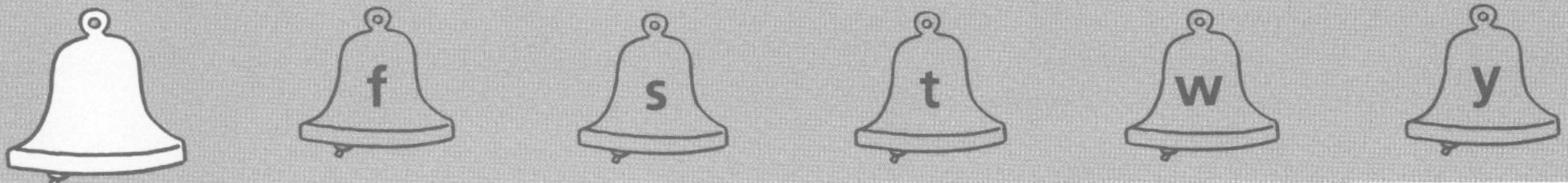 **f**	**s**	**t**	**w**	**y**

bull	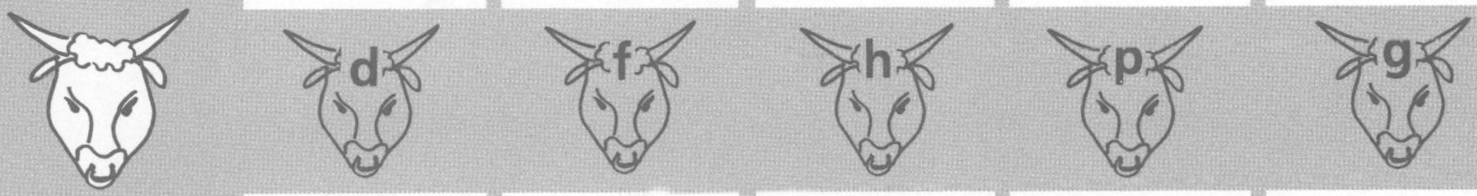 **d**	**f**	**h**	**p**	**g**

Add 'll' to make a word.

se	ll
fe	
du	
do	
be	

Now use the words in these sentences.

I ___fell___ in the playground.

I play with my _____ .

I heard the _____ ring.

Florists _____ flowers.

It is a _____ day.

Write the words for the pictures in the word wall.

	well			

Write Read Learn Spell

bull bell call tell doll fell full well hall pull

In your exercise book write ten sentences using these words.

Join the letters to make a new word.

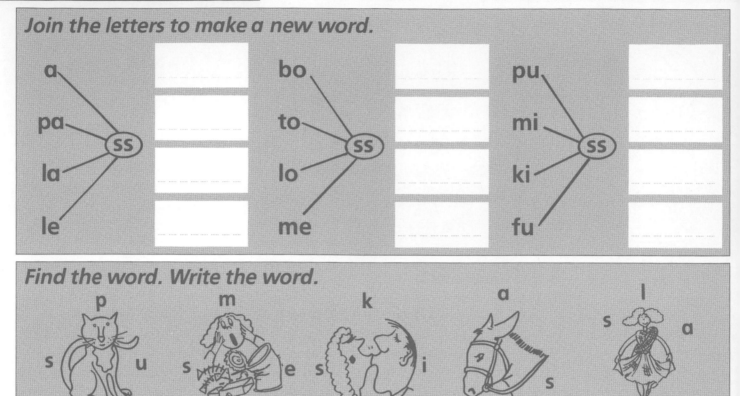

a
pa
la → ss
le

bo
to
lo → ss
me

pu
mi
ki → ss
fu

Find the word. Write the word.

p
s   u
s

m
s   e
s

k
s   i
s

a
s

l
s   a
s

Complete the puzzle using the words you have made.

A cat. → . . .

Untidy – a . . .

I am in charge. → . . .

A lot of bother. → . . .

T   and turn.

Not a donkey. → . . .

I like playing . . . the parcel.

Write Read Learn Spell

pass less miss kiss fuss boss toss loss puss mess

In your exercise book write ten sentences using these words.

Make new words. Write the words.

o   cu   hu   pu   bu   fu

ff   **zz**

| | | | | | | |

Complete the sentences using the words you have made.

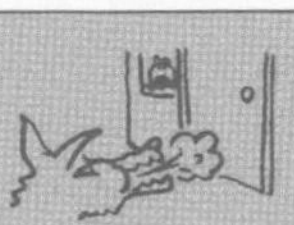

The wolf said I'll _____ and I'll _____ and I'll blow your house down.

A shirt sleeve has a _____ .   Jump _____ the wall.

The bees _____ round the flowers.

Write   Read   Learn   Spell

off   cuff   huff   puff   buzz   fuzz

In your exercise book write six sentences using these words.

Can you remember?   – ff – ll – ss   **Complete the puzzle.**

I can catch a . . . .

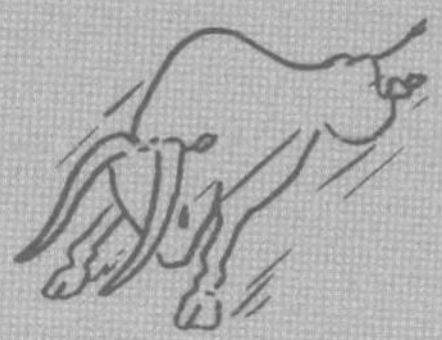

Don't . . . over.

The . . . rang.

A seaside bird. → . . . .

I will . . . you.

We . . . the shops on the way.

Turn . . . the light.

I saw a . . . of smoke.

. . . the hoop down the hill.

Some shops . . . food.

Children play with a . . . .

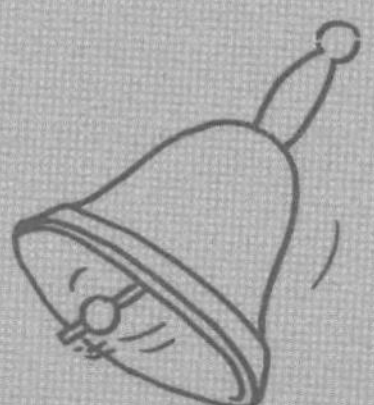

Not a cow → . . . .

b			
f			
b			
g			
m			
p			
p			
r			
s			
d			
b			

Make new words. Write the words.

sa
ba — ck
pa

___sack___

ne
pe — ck
de

wi
pi — ck
li

so
lo — ck
co

du
tu — ck
su

Write the word.

r
k   a
c

d
k   e
c

t
k   i
c

r
k   o
c

l
k   u
c

___rack___   d_____   t_____   r_____   l_____

Complete the puzzle.

1. . . . your bag.
2. Not the front. → . . .
3.
4. Birds . . . seeds.
5. A clock says . . . -tock.
6.
7.
8. It keeps your foot warm.
9. We have a . . . shop.
10. Babies . . . their fingers.

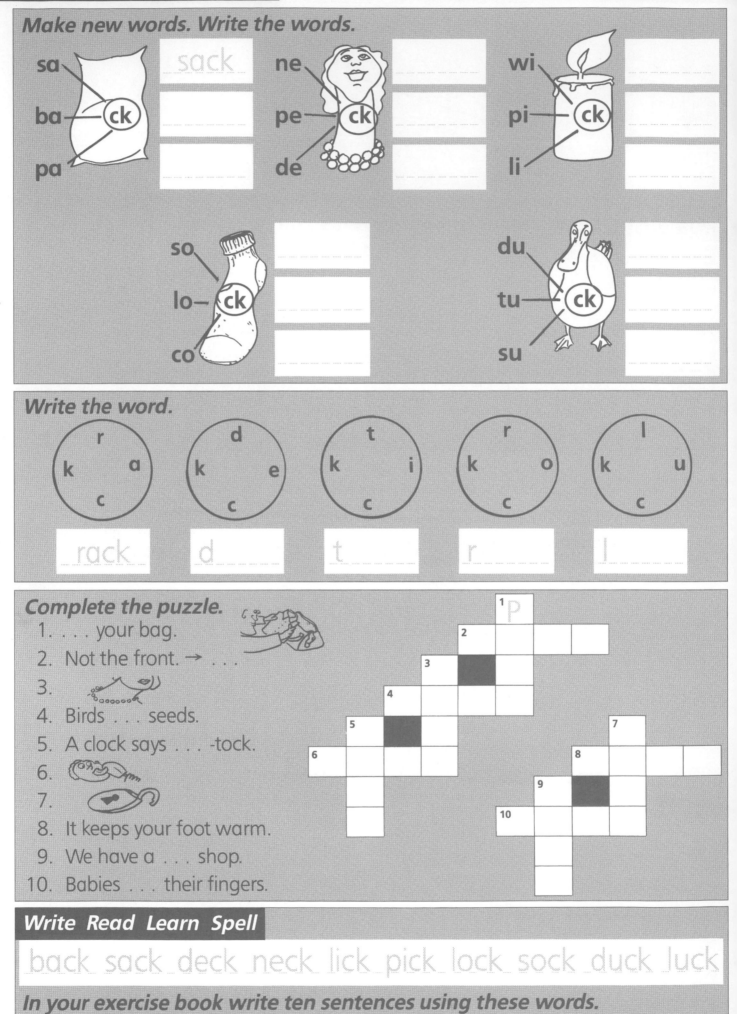

back sack deck neck lick pick lock sock duck luck

In your exercise book write ten sentences using these words.

Make new words. Write the words.

ki		king
ri		
wi	ng	
si		
di		

ba		
sa		
ha	ng	
ra		
ga		

hu		
ru		
su	ng	
lu		
bu		

| lo | go | so | do |

ng

Complete the puzzle.

1.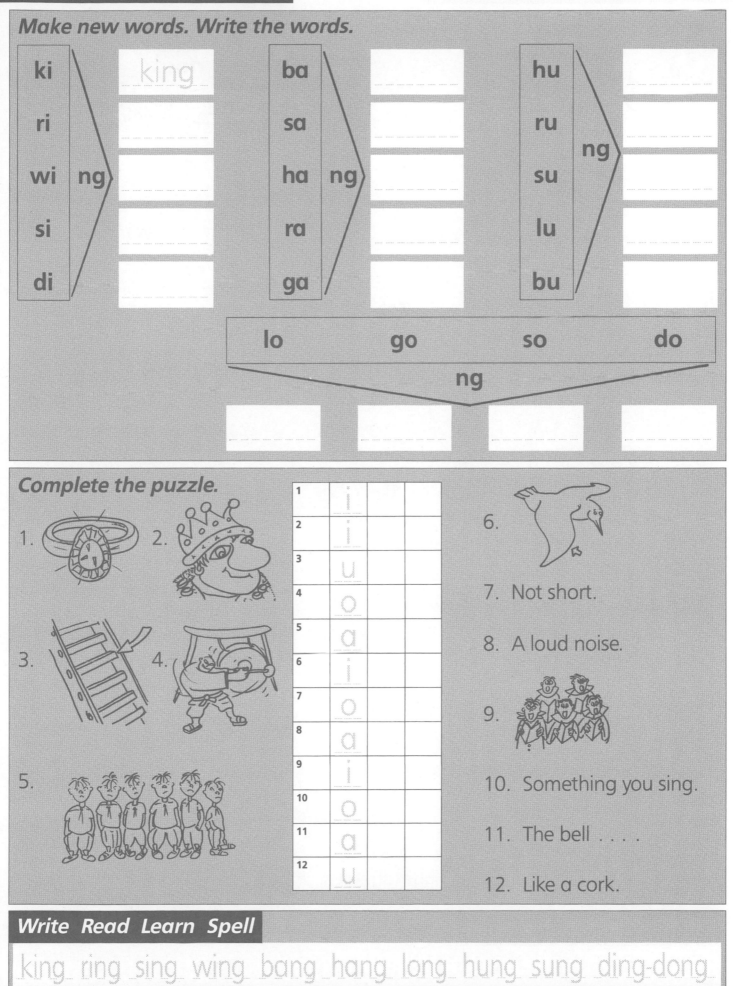
2.
3.
4.
5.

1	i		
2	i		
3	u		
4	o		
5	a		
6	i		
7	o		
8	a		
9	i		
10	o		
11	a		
12	u		

6.

7. Not short.

8. A loud noise.

9.

10. Something you sing.

11. The bell . . . .

12. Like a cork.

Write Read Learn Spell

king ring sing wing bang hang long hung sung ding-dong

In your exercise book write ten sentences using these words.

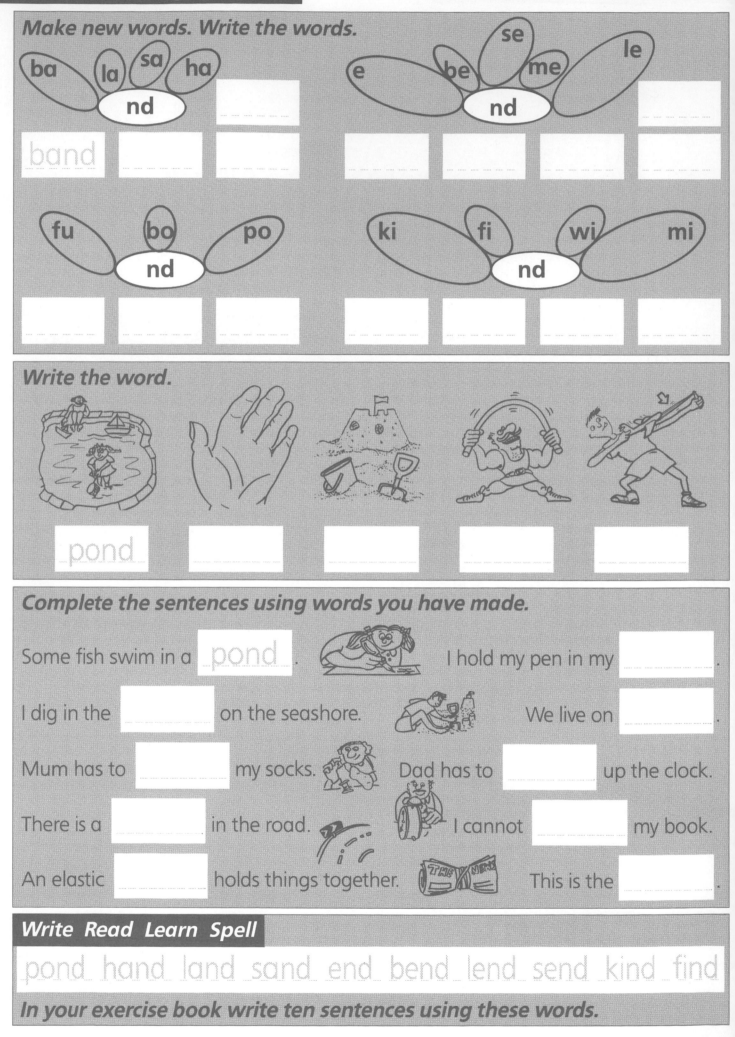

Make new words. Write the words.

ba   la   sa   ha
nd

band

e   be   se   me   le
nd

fu   bo   po
nd

ki   fi   wi   mi
nd

Write the word.

_pond

Complete the sentences using words you have made.

Some fish swim in a _pond .

I hold my pen in my _____ .

I dig in the _____ on the seashore.

We live on _____ .

Mum has to _____ my socks.

Dad has to _____ up the clock.

There is a _____ in the road.

I cannot _____ my book.

An elastic _____ holds things together.

This is the _____ .

Write Read Learn Spell

pond hand land sand end bend lend send kind find

In your exercise book write ten sentences using these words.

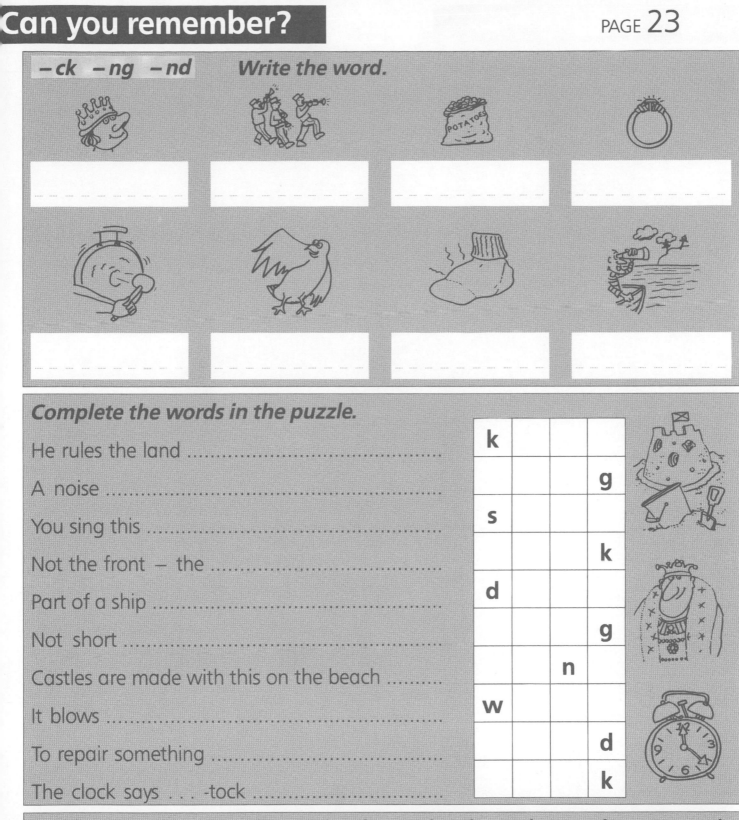

– ck – ng – nd   Write the word.

Complete the words in the puzzle.

He rules the land ....

A noise ....

You sing this ....

Not the front – the ....

Part of a ship ....

Not short ....

Castles are made with this on the beach ....

It blows ....

To repair something ....

The clock says . . . -tock ....

k			
			g
s			
			k
d			
			g
		n	
w			
			d
			k

Find six words in the snake. The last letter of each word starts the new word.

Write the words below.

1. hand   2. _____   3. _____   4. _____   5. _____   6. _____

In your exercise book use five of these words in sentences.

Pets

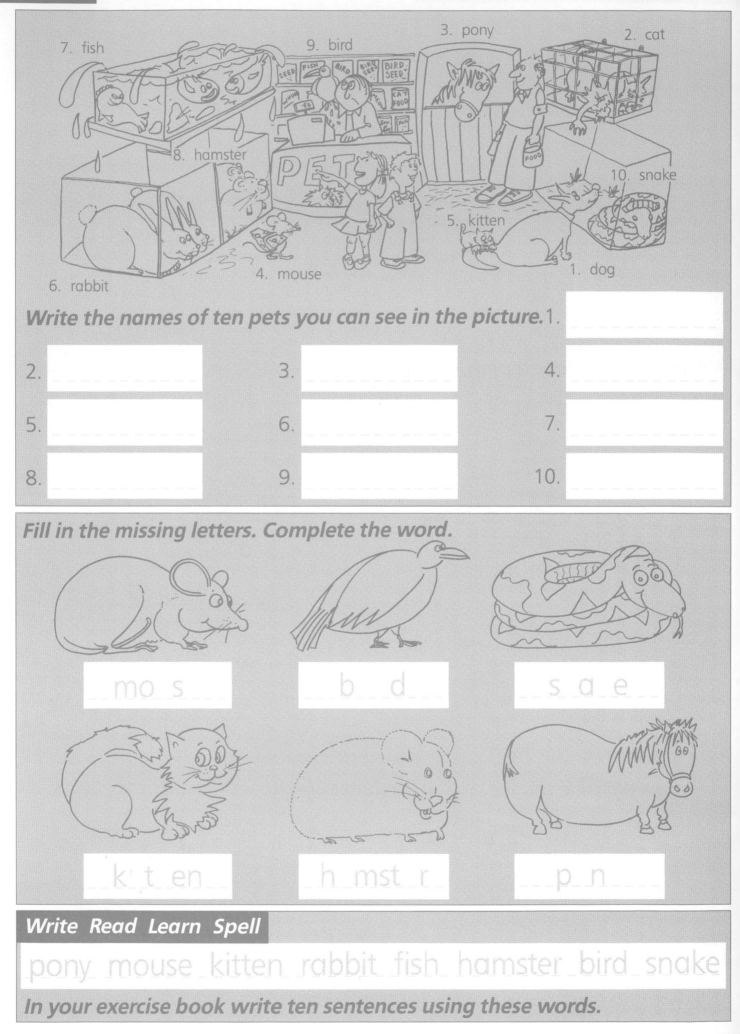

7. fish
9. bird
3. pony
2. cat
8. hamster
10. snake
5. kitten
4. mouse
1. dog
6. rabbit

Write the names of ten pets you can see in the picture.

1.

2.

3.

4.

5.

6.

7.

8.

9.

10.

Fill in the missing letters. Complete the word.

_ mo _ s _

b _ d

s _ a _ e _

_ k _ t _ en _

h _ mst _ r

_ p _ n _

Write Read Learn Spell

pony mouse kitten rabbit fish hamster bird snake

In your exercise book write ten sentences using these words.

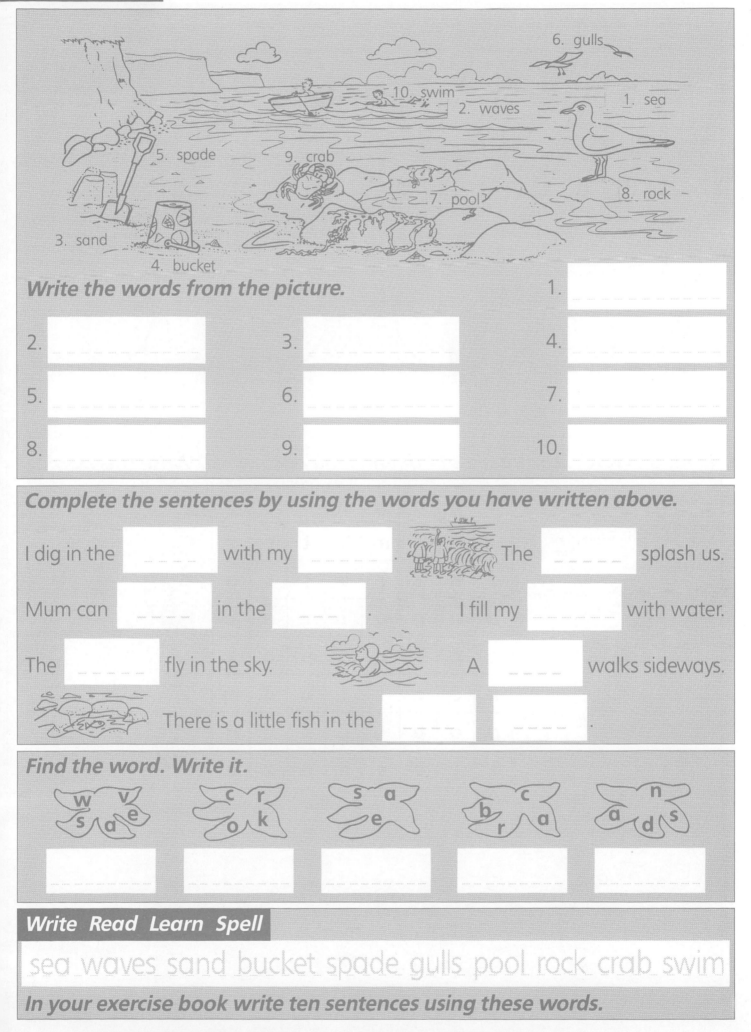

6. gulls

10. swim

2. waves

1. sea

5. spade

9. crab

8. rock

7. pool

3. sand

4. bucket

Write the words from the picture.

1.

2.

3.

4.

5.

6.

7.

8.

9.

10.

Complete the sentences by using the words you have written above.

I dig in the _____ with my _____ . The _____ splash us.

Mum can _____ in the _____ . I fill my _____ with water.

The _____ fly in the sky. A _____ walks sideways.

There is a little fish in the _____ _____ .

Find the word. Write it.

w v e
s a

c r
o k

s a
e

c
b a
r

n
a s
d

Write Read Learn Spell

sea waves sand bucket spade gulls pool rock crab swim

In your exercise book write ten sentences using these words.

Pets and the seashore. Write the word.

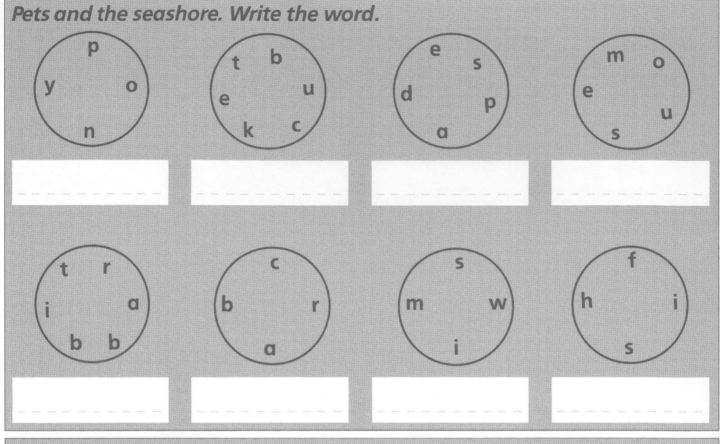

Find ten words. Look across or down. Ring each word. Write the word.

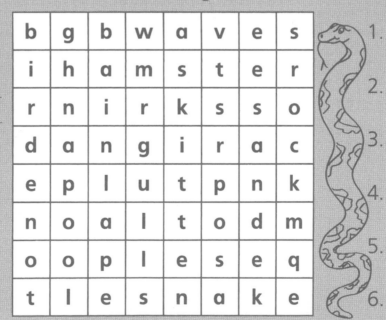

b	g	b	w	a	v	e	s
i	h	a	m	s	t	e	r
r	n	i	r	k	s	s	o
d	a	n	g	i	r	a	c
e	p	l	u	t	p	n	k
n	o	a	l	t	o	d	m
o	o	p	l	e	s	e	q
t	l	e	s	n	a	k	e

1.

2.

3.

4.

5.

6.

7.

8.

9.

10.

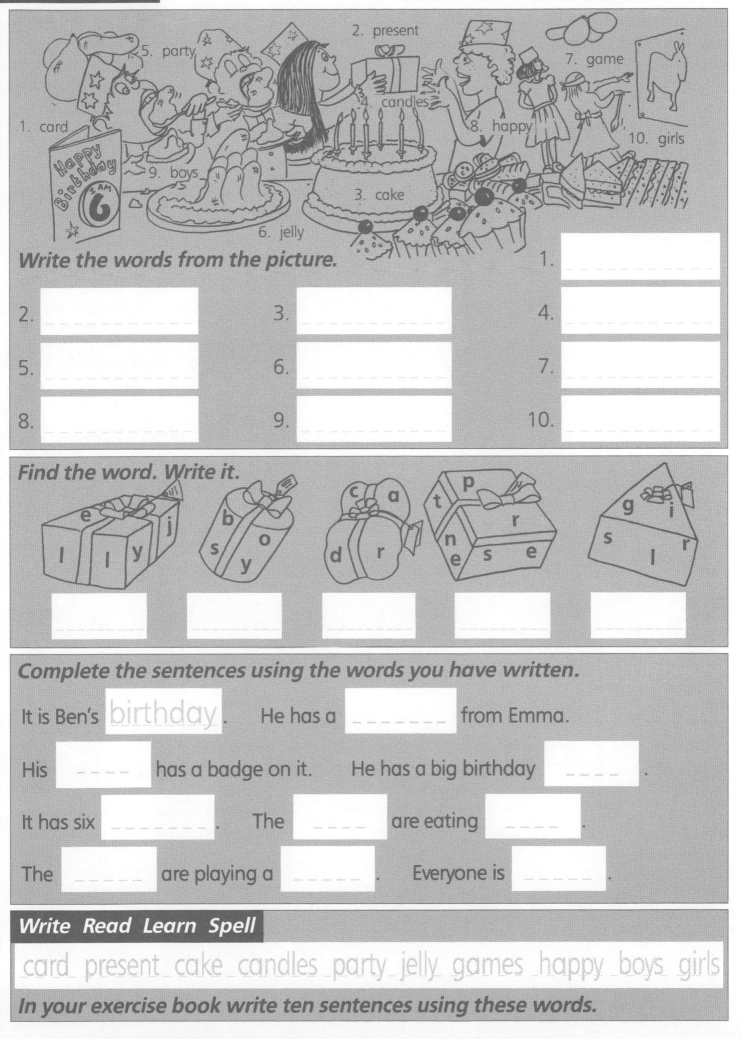

Write the words from the picture.

1. _____

2. _____

3. _____

4. _____

5. _____

6. _____

7. _____

8. _____

9. _____

10. _____

Find the word. Write it.

_____   _____   _____   _____   _____

Complete the sentences using the words you have written.

It is Ben's birthday.   He has a _____ from Emma.

His _____ has a badge on it.   He has a big birthday _____.

It has six _____.   The _____ are eating _____.

The _____ are playing a _____.   Everyone is _____.

Write Read Learn Spell

card present cake candles party jelly games happy boys girls

In your exercise book write ten sentences using these words.

How many? Look at the picture. Write the number word.

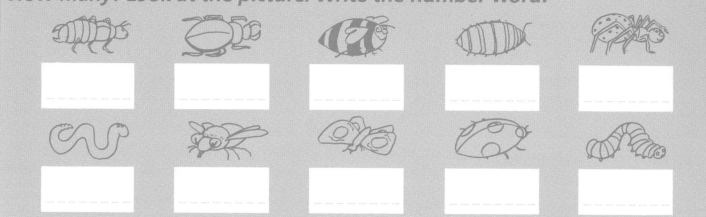

Complete the puzzle.

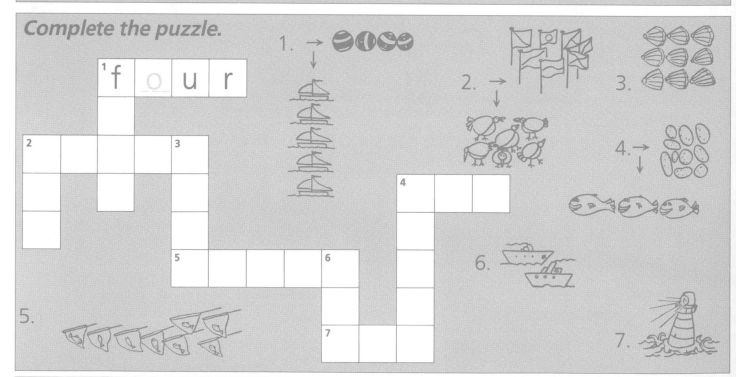

1. f o u r

In your exercise book write ten sentences using these words.

Complete the puzzle.

1. Not down.

2.

3.

4. You play . . .at a party.

5.

6.

7.

8.

9. A knock . . .the door.

10. Not out.

11. Not she.

12. Not off.

13.

14. . . . are going to school.

15. ↓ The flower . . . red.

16.

17. Not on.

18. A cup . . .tea.

Schofield&Sims

the long-established educational publisher
specialising in maths, English and science materials for schools

Early Spelling is a series of graded activity books that helps children to learn key spelling patterns through puzzles and other activities.

Early Spelling Book 1 covers:

- Short vowel sounds in words
- Word endings (for example, 'll', 'ff', 'ck' and 'ng')
- Number words.

This book is suitable for children making the transition from the Early Years Foundation Stage to Key Stage 1 and those already in Key Stage 1 who need further practice.

The full range of titles in the series is as follows:

Early Spelling Book 1:   ISBN 978 07217 0838 6

Early Spelling Book 2:   ISBN 978 07217 0839 3

Early Spelling Book 3:   ISBN 978 07217 0840 9

Have you tried **First Phonics** by Schofield & Sims?
This series of books helps children to learn the sounds, spelling patterns and word-building skills necessary for reading and writing.

**For further information and to place your order
visit www.schofieldandsims.co.uk or telephone 01484 607080**

ISBN 978-07217-0838-6

9 780721 708386

Schofield&Sims

Dogley Mill, Fenay Bridge, Huddersfield HD8 0NQ
Phone: 01484 607080 Facsimile: 01484 606815
E-mail: sales@schofieldandsims.co.uk
www.schofieldandsims.co.uk

ISBN 978 07217 0838 6

**£2.45
(Retail price)**

Key Stage 1
Age range: 5–7 years

KS-844-072

What is exaggeration?

Exaggeration occurs when a fact or a piece of information is distorted in some way – stretching the truth. People are often guilty of exaggeration in their day-to-day lives. For example, football supporters often claim that their team is the best in the land when in fact they are situated halfway up the league table. This is an exaggerated statement.

SUMMARY

Bias is found in many sources used in Modern Studies. Bias means to take a one-sided viewpoint.

Exaggeration is also a problem when studying sources of information. Exaggeration means to stretch the truth.

ACTIVITIES

Read the two newspaper reports in Figure **B**, which describe the same event, and then answer the questions that follow.

Figure B

Extracts from *The Globe* and *The Echo*

The Globe

Prime Minister Delivers Brilliant Speech at Blues Party Conference

The Prime Minister yesterday delivered a brilliant speech to the party's annual conference. In his speech the Prime Minister outlined his party's successes in government over the last 4 years. More hospitals and schools have been built, more police officers have been put on Britain's streets and fewer people are unemployed than there were 4 years ago. A masterful performance from a truly outstanding leader.

THE ECHO

Prime Minister Fails to Deliver the Goods at Blues Party Conference

The Prime Minister failed to provide much hope for the British public at yesterday's Blues Annual Party Conference. The Prime Minister failed to inspire party supporters when he outlined the Blues' poor record on health, education and law and order. A weak speech from a poor leader and one which will please all Reds supporters.

1 Study the newspaper report from *The Globe*. Write down three words or phrases which clearly show that *The Globe* is biased in favour of the Prime Minister.

2 Study the newspaper report from *The Echo*. Write down three words or phrases which clearly show that *The Echo* is biased against the Prime Minister.

3 Study Table **C**.

Table C

British people's holidays abroad by destination in 2000

Country	%	Country	%
Spain	28	Belgium	2
France	18	Germany	2
Greece	7	Netherlands	2
United States	7	Turkey	2
Irish Republic	5	Austria	1
Italy	4	Malta	1
Portugal	4	Other countries	14
Cyprus	3		

(a) 'Most British people went on holiday to Spain in 2000.'
Travel agency spokesperson

What evidence is there in Table **C** to suggest that the travel agency spokesperson is exaggerating?

(b) 'Belgium is the least popular holiday destination for British people.'
Travel agency spokesperson

What evidence is there in Table **C** to suggest that the travel agency spokesperson is exaggerating?

4 'Newspapers should not be allowed to support political parties.'
Do you agree with this statement?
Provide arguments to support your view.

1.4 What is inaccurate information?

Using different types of information

It is important when we handle sources of information in Modern Studies that we are able to spot information that is inaccurate.

Stereotypes

Stereotypes are one reason for inaccurate sources of information. A **stereotype** is a generalisation. Racial stereotyping is very common, for example. Racial stereotyping leads to a lot of inaccurate information about people in society.

A **racial stereotype** is a view about a racial group that is based on very crude generalisations, not on facts.

Perhaps the most common type of stereotyping that takes place is racial. Many people hold mental pictures or attitudes towards some racial groups which are simply not based on facts. They are based on generalisations and viewpoints which are fixed.

Scots are a racial group that is often stereotyped. The classic stereotypical view of a Scot is one who has ginger hair, is frequently drunk, aggressive, and invariably wears a kilt.

Racial stereotyping is not confined to the past. In modern Britain there are still many people who hold stereotypical racial views. Indeed, such views are a part of everyday life. Racial stereotyping can lead to **prejudice, discrimination** and sometimes even **persecution.** People who are prejudiced against others hold negative views about certain types of people just because they see them as stereotypes. Discrimination often leads on from persecution and occurs when groups are denied the same opportunities as everyone else in society. Persecution occurs when people are deliberately made to suffer because of prejudiced views about them.

Study Figure , which examines how racial stereotyping can lead to persecution.

Figure A

NAZI TREATMENT OF JEWS
Adolf Hitler became leader of Germany in 1933. At this time many Germans were unemployed and living in poverty. Hitler viewed German Jews as one of the main causes of Germany's problems. He believed that all Jews were sub-human and mentally and physically inferior to non-Jews. He used radio, cinema and demonstrations to highlight what he called the 'Jewish Problem'. Many Germans believed Hitler's mental picture of Jews and discriminated against them by refusing to buy goods from Jewish shops. Hitler passed laws which banned Jewish children from attending schools and stopped Jews marrying non-Jews. Then during the Second World War, he ordered the mass killing of Jews in Central and Eastern Europe. By 1945 around 6 million Jews had been murdered.

Selective use of the facts

Information also becomes inaccurate when people only select facts to support their point of view. In other words, they ignore information. This is called selective use of the facts.

Read the following statement:

> The Church of England is the only religion people in Great Britain belong to.

Study Table and think of reasons why this statement is selective in the use of the facts.

Table

Percentage of people in Britain belonging to a religion in 2000

People were asked: 'Do you regard yourself as belonging to any particular religion?'

Religion	%
Church of England	29.9
Roman Catholic	9.2
Christian – no denomination	6.3
Presbyterian/Free Presbyterian/Church of Scotland	3.6
Baptist or Methodist	3.4
Other Protestant	2.5
United Reform Church	0.5
Muslim	2.0
Hindu	1.0
Jewish	0.8
Sikh	0.4
Buddhist	0.1
Don't know	0.7
No religion	39.6

The person who made the statement at the top of the page can be accused of being selective in the use of the facts because the Church of England is clearly not the *only* religion that people in Britain belong to. For example, 9.2% of British people said they were Roman Catholic.

SUMMARY

Stereotypes are a problem when we examine sources of information in Modern Studies.

Stereotypes are not based on facts, but are based on a person's attitude and mental picture of individuals or groups.

Racial stereotypes can be damaging. They can lead to prejudice, discrimination and persecution.

Information is also sometimes highly selective. People who are selective in their use of the facts leave out vital pieces of information that don't support their point of view.

ACTIVITIES

1 What is a *stereotype*?

2 Can you think of any racial stereotypes other than those described here?

3 Read Figure Ⓐ. Give an example of prejudice, discrimination and persecution described in Figure Ⓐ.

4 Why is racial stereotyping damaging?

5 'Britain has only a few religions.'
   Look at Table Ⓑ. Why can the person making this statement be accused of being selective in the use of the facts?

6 Can you think of any instances when people in everyday life are selective in their use of facts?

2.1 What do we mean by rules and laws?

Rules and laws control the way people behave in a society. The terms *rules* and *laws* are used in very similar ways but there are important differences in what each word actually means.

Rules

A rule is a standard which individuals are expected to follow. Many organisations have made rules that members must follow. For example, schools have their own set of rules which pupils are expected not to break. Study Figure , which shows the set of rules that apply to Castle High School:

Figure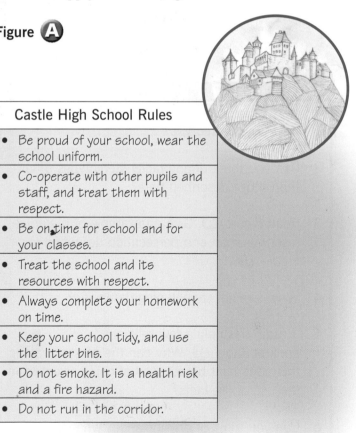

Castle High School Rules
• Be proud of your school, wear the school uniform.
• Co-operate with other pupils and staff, and treat them with respect.
• Be on time for school and for your classes.
• Treat the school and its resources with respect.
• Always complete your homework on time.
• Keep your school tidy, and use the litter bins.
• Do not smoke. It is a health risk and a fire hazard.
• Do not run in the corridor.

Castle High School's set of rules are fairly typical of school rules in most parts of Scotland. School rules are created for two main reasons:

1 To protect pupils and ensure their safety.

2 To ensure that order is maintained and that every pupil is aware of a common set of rules which apply to their behaviour.

It is not just schools that have rules. Sports such as bowling, rugby, football and golf all have a set of rules which members are expected to follow. Can you imagine a game of football without any rules?

Laws

Although rules and laws are very similar, there are some important differences.

■ The main difference between a rule and a law is that a law is something that society takes very seriously. Most societies have set up a whole system based around laws. For example, the police make sure that people don't break the law and the courts deal with people who are accused of breaking the law.

■ Golf clubs, swimming pools and your parents can make rules, but only a few organisations can make laws. Laws that affect Scotland are made either by the British Parliament, based in London, or by the Scottish Parliament, based in Edinburgh. Local councils also have the power to make some laws.

Like rules, laws are in place to protect people in society. Laws also ensure that order is maintained in society.

In 1948, the ship *Empire Windrush* brought 482 immigrants from Jamaica to Britain. ▶

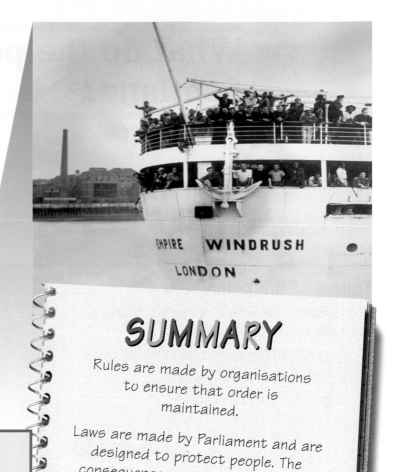

Changes to rules and laws

Rules and laws are not fixed. They often change in response to different circumstances. The law is changing all the time and this is often in response to changing circumstances in society.

For example, since the 1950s Britain has witnessed the large-scale **immigration** of people from Commonwealth countries such as India, Pakistan and the West Indies. These people have moved to Britain in search of a better life.

The Race Relations Act was passed in 1976 by Parliament to make it an offence to discriminate against people because they are from a different race. This is an example of the law changing in response to wider changes in society.

SUMMARY

Rules are made by organisations to ensure that order is maintained.

Laws are made by Parliament and are designed to protect people. The consequences are more serious for breaking a law than for breaking a rule.

Rules and laws can change over time.

ACTIVITIES

1   Describe what makes a *law* different from a *rule*.

2   Why are rules and laws necessary?

3   Look at Figure Ⓐ. Can you think of any rules in your school that are different from those in Figure Ⓐ?

4   Copy the following table into your notebook:

Rule	Law

Sort this list of rules and laws into your table:
■ *No running in the corridor*
■ *Motorway speed limit 70 mph*
■ *Offside in a football match*
■ *No jeans to be worn in local sports club*
■ *Foxhunting in Scotland is banned*
■ *The Race Relations Act*

5   Who makes laws?

6   Try to find out about any new laws made recently in the British and Scottish Parliaments.

7   'Laws never change.'
    Do you agree with this statement?
    Give examples to back up your argument.

70 MPH

2.2 What do the police do in Scotland?

What the police do

The police do not *make* the laws in Scotland. They merely *enforce* the law. In other words, the police arrest individuals whom they suspect have broken the law.

Duties of the police

The duties of the police can be summarised like this:

- To prevent offences (crimes) taking place
- To maintain order in society
- To protect law and property.

Powers of the police

The police have a number of important powers. Study Diagram **A**.

Diagram A

Arrest

Police officers can arrest someone who has carried out a crime or whom the police suspect has carried out a crime.

Search

Individuals who are arrested by the police may be searched. Premises may also be searched if the police obtain a Search Warrant.

Gather evidence

A police officer may gather evidence such as fingerprints or palmprints. In some cases the police collect hairs or blood samples from suspects. This allows the police to match DNA taken from crime scenes, to suspects.

POWERS OF THE POLICE

Detention

A police officer in Scotland may detain a suspect to enable investigations to take place. Suspects can only be detained for 6 hours. After 6 hours the police must either release or arrest the suspect.

How well are the police performing?

One way of measuring how well the police are performing is to examine **clear-up rates**. Clear-up rates show the percentage of crimes successfully cleared-up by the police. Clear-up rates vary depending on the crime. Study Table **B**.

Table **B**

Clear-up rates in Scotland as a percentage of those recorded in selected crimes: 1990, 1995 and 1999

Crime	Year		
	1990	1995	1999
Serious assault	65	54	64
Robbery	28	29	38
Theft of a motor vehicle	24	24	32

Police clear-up rates are one way in which the public judge the performance of the police. In general, the majority of the public believe that the police are doing a good job. Study Table **C**.

Table **C**

Percentage satisfaction with the police, 2000

Attitudes	Would you say that the police in this area do a good job or a poor job?
Very good	14
Fairly good	57
Fairly poor	13
Very poor	4
Don't know	12

SUMMARY

The police are responsible for enforcing the law. They have the power of arrest, detention, search and evidence-gathering to help them.

Recent surveys show that the public are generally satisfied with the work of the police in Scotland.

ACTIVITIES

1   In groups, or with the person sitting next to you, write down as many reasons as possible why people break the law.

2   Describe the duties of the police.

3   Describe in detail the main powers of the police.

4   'The police do a good job in Scotland.' Use the evidence in Tables **B** and **C** to support this view.

5   Design a poster encouraging young people in your area to join the police. Your poster should include:
   ■ what the police do
   ■ why this is important in the community.

2.3 What do courts do in Scotland?

After the police have arrested and charged a suspect, a case is prepared against the accused by the **Procurator Fiscal**. The Procurator Fiscal is responsible for carrying out the prosecution of accused people in courts. Those who are accused of a crime and stand trial are entitled to a defence lawyer. The defence lawyer tries to prove the innocence of the accused before a judge and jury. The Scottish legal system has its own courts, which are quite different from the rest of the United Kingdom (UK). However, one similarity between Scottish courts and those in the rest of the UK is the split between **civil courts** and **criminal courts**.

Civil courts

Civil courts deal with disputes between individuals and organisations. Issues such as marriage, divorce, property rights and the custody of children are dealt with by civil courts.

Diagram

The criminal court structure in Scotland

More serious offences

High Court of the Justiciary

Sheriff Court

District Court

Less serious offences

Criminal courts

Criminal courts are concerned with crimes against the community which endanger its well-being, such as theft, robbery, drug dealing and murder. In criminal courts the state – on behalf of citizens of the country – prosecutes individuals who have broken the law.

The criminal court system in Scotland

There are three main types of criminal court in Scotland: the **District Court**, the **Sheriff Court** and the **High Court of the Justiciary**. The District and Sheriff Courts deal with less serious offences than the High Court. Diagram **A** illustrates this.

The High Court of the Justiciary

The highest criminal court in Scotland is the High Court of the Justiciary. The High Court sits in four areas of Scotland at various times. These four areas are called circuits. For example, the Home Circuit is based in Edinburgh, whilst Glasgow is the busiest city in the West Circuit. Sittings of the North Circuit often take place in Inverness and Aberdeen, while Dumfries and Ayr have been used by the South Circuit. Serious offences such as murder, armed robbery and drug dealing are tried in the High Court. A judge controls what happens in the High Court and decides on a suitable sentence after a jury of 15 decide on the guilt of the accused.

The Sheriff Court

Sheriff Courts are located in Scotland's main towns and cities. In some cases the Sheriff judges the case without a jury. These are called **summary cases**. Summary cases include theft and minor drug offences.

Sheriff Courts also deal with solemn cases. These are more serious offences and a jury is used to decide on the guilt of the accused person. The sentence handed out by Sheriff Courts is not as serious as those given by the High Court.

▲ A Scottish judge.

SUMMARY

The Procurator Fiscal has responsibility for prosecuting those accused of committing crimes in Scotland.

Accused persons are entitled to defence lawyers.

Civil law concerns disputes between people. Criminal law cases concern crimes against society.

In Scotland there are three main criminal courts: The High Court of the Justiciary, Sheriff Courts and District Courts.

The District Court

Scotland has 56 District Courts which are based in the major towns and cities. District Courts are the lowest courts in Scotland and deal with minor crimes such as breach of the peace. A **Justice of the Peace** (JP) controls and decides upon the guilt of an accused person in a District Court. JPs are not legally qualified. District Courts cannot hand out sentences that are as serious as those dealt with by the High Court and Sheriff Courts.

ACTIVITY

Write a report that describes the court structure in Scotland. Use the following headings
- *Civil courts*
- *Criminal courts*
- *Procurator Fiscal*
- *Defence*
- *High Court*
- *Sheriff Court*
- *District Court*

2.4 How does the Children's Hearing System work?

The Children's Hearing System

In Scotland the **Children's Hearing System** has been developed to deal with children under the age of 16 who break the law or are in need of special care and protection.

The Children's Hearing System has been created as an alternative to children appearing before criminal courts in Scotland.

Who is brought before the Children's Hearing System?

It is unusual for children under the age of 16 to be prosecuted in a criminal court. Only in cases where children have committed serious offences such as murder does this happen. In other cases children are brought before the Children's Hearing System. Children appear before the Children's Hearing System for a number of reasons:

- Where children are beyond the control of their parents or guardian
- Where children are exposed to moral danger
- Where a child has been the victim of an offence, including physical or sexual abuse
- Where a child's health is likely to suffer as a result of a lack of parental care
- Where a child is involved in solvent abuse, misusing drugs or alcohol
- Where a child has committed an offence
- Where a child has failed to attend school without a reasonable excuse.

What is a Children's Panel?

Children can be referred to the Children's Hearing System by any member of the public. However, it is usually organisations such as the police, social services and education departments that refer children. The **Reporter** is the name given to the person who decides whether a child should be referred to the Children's Hearing System. The Reporter weighs up all the evidence before making this decision.

Children who are referred to the Hearing System appear before a panel of three people – this is called a Children's Panel. There must be both men and women on the panel – so there couldn't be three men, or three women. Panel members are trained to deal with children and their families.

What happens at a Children's Panel?

Children usually attend their own panel meeting. As well as the three panel members, the child's parents or guardian also attend. Members of the press may also be present, and there is usually a member of the Children's Panel Advisory Committee (CPAC) in attendance. This person's job is to monitor the role of panel members.

Panel hearings usually take place around a table. Panel members receive reports on children from the social services department and the school. Medical and psychiatric reports can also be asked for.

At the panel meeting the child's circumstances are discussed fully. The child has the opportunity to speak at any time in the meeting.

After they have considered the evidence, the panel members make a decision on what should happen next. The decision will be their view of what will be best for the child in the long term.

What powers do Children's Panels have?

Panels have a number of powers. They can remove a child from his or her home to a children's home, a residential school or secure accommodation, if they decide this would best protect the child. The Panel could decide to place a child with foster parents. Often children are kept with their parents under the supervision of a social worker.

Children's Panels do not have the power to fine children or their parents.

SUMMARY

The Children's Hearing System has developed in Scotland for children under 16 who break the law or are in need of special care and protection.

Children can be referred to a Children's Panel.

A Children's Panel has a number of powers. For example, the Children's Panel has the power to place children who are at risk, with foster parents.

ACTIVITIES

1   List four reasons why children could appear before the Children's Hearing System.

2   Who can refer children to the Children's Hearing System?

3   Why do you think the three Children's Panel members cannot all be men or all be women?

4   What happens at a Children's Panel?

5   Do you think that the Children's Panel is a good way of helping children in trouble? Explain your answer.

6   'The Children's Panel has no power.' Provide evidence to show that this statement is inaccurate.

2.5 How do we measure crime?

Measuring crime

Statistics which measure the amount of crime that takes place in Scotland are mostly based on reported crimes. **Reported crimes** are offences that have been reported to the police. There is a problem in only using statistics that are based on reported crimes because many crimes take place that are not reported to the police. There are two main reasons for this:

- People do not report crimes that are trivial. For example, many minor thefts are not reported because the victim does not think that the theft is important enough to contact the police.

- Many people are frightened to report certain crimes that have taken place. Some victims are intimidated by criminals.

When we examine criminal activity it is important to remember that the official statistics produced by the government may only tell part of the story.
The main way that **unreported crimes** are measured in Scotland is through the Scottish Crime Survey (SCS). The SCS takes place every four years and attempts to find out the number of unreported crimes in Scotland.

Diagram (A)

Crimes recorded in Scotland, 2001

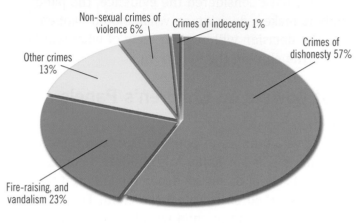

Non-sexual crimes of violence 6%
Crimes of indecency 1%
Crimes of dishonesty 57%
Other crimes 13%
Fire-raising, and vandalism 23%

Crime trends in Scotland

Diagram (A) shows the main types of crimes recorded in Scotland in 2001.

As you can see from Diagram (A), crimes of dishonesty accounted for the largest percentage of crimes in Scotland in 2001. The types of crime committed under this category mainly relate to theft. For example, in 2001 there were almost 45,000 recorded crimes of housebreaking and attempted housebreaking.

The total number of crimes recorded by the police in Scotland was 421,000. This was a reduction from the previous year. The total number of offences recorded was almost 525,000. **Offences** relate to less serious criminal acts than crimes. For example, many minor breaches in motoring law, like speeding, are considered offences. Serious assault is an example of a crime.

One of the most worrying crime trends in the last 10 years or so has been the dramatic increase in drug-related crimes. Diagram (B) shows the number of crimes recorded for possession of drugs between 1992 and 2001.

◀ Police may detain fans if they cause a disturbance at a football match.

Diagram B

Possession of drugs reported by the police, 1992–2001

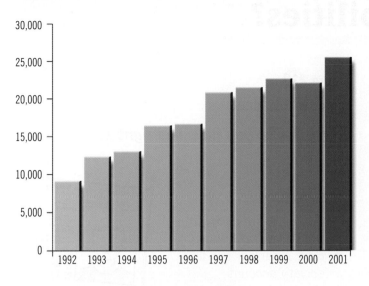

Knife carrying in Scotland

One of the most alarming crime trends in recent years in Scotland relates to the number of assaults that have taken place where a knife has been involved. Many murders take place as a result of individuals carrying knives. Read Figure C, which is an extract from a newspaper report describing this problem.

Figure C

From *Scotland on Sunday*, 29 September 2002

SCOTLAND'S SCHOOLGIRLS ARMED AND DANGEROUS

One in seven 14-year-old girls carries a knife or other weapon, according to disturbing new research which suggests young Scottish women are embracing the country's culture of violence.

And despite concerted attempts by the government and police to stamp out the menace, a third of boys of the same age also carry a knife.

More than 4,000 Scots are being tracked by research carried out by the University of Edinburgh which started in 1998, from the age of 12 to 30.

The youngsters are regularly questioned on a range of crime-related issues, including whether they carry a weapon. The survey asked youngsters: 'Have you carried a knife or weapon for protection or in case it was needed in a fight?'

At the age of 13 it emerged that a quarter of boys were carrying a knife or other weapon, typically a baseball bat or hammer. Only 7% of girls said they carried a weapon.

When the girls reached the age of 14 it emerged that the carrying of knives and other weapons had doubled to 14%. Among the boys, the figure had increased to 32%. The most recent survey, carried out when the group reached 15, suggests that 14 is the peak age for knife carrying. A year later the figure for boys had dropped marginally to 30% and for girls was down to 10%. Somewhere between 20% and 30% of gang members are girls.

SUMMARY

Reported crimes are recorded by the police. Many crimes are unreported.

The largest category of crime in Scotland in 2001 was those related to dishonesty.

There has been a dramatic increase in drug- and knife-related crime in recent years.

ACTIVITIES

1 Why do some victims not report crimes to the police?

2 Why does relying on reported crimes not give the full picture of criminal activity in Scotland?

3 Study Diagram A. Describe the main patterns of crime in Scotland.

4 What evidence is there in Diagram B to show that drugs are an increasing problem?

5 Read the newspaper article in Figure C.
   (a) What evidence is there that knife carrying is on the increase?
   (b) What evidence is there that girls are involved in gangs?
   (c) 'Every girl in Scotland carries a knife.' Why is this statement an exaggeration?

3.1 What do we mean by rights and responsibilities?

Children in Scotland are born with certain **rights**. As they grow older, the number of legal rights they can claim increases substantially.

What are legal rights?

A **legal right** is something that people can claim by law. The law makes sure that people's legal rights are upheld. The idea of giving citizens of a country rights is not a new one. An early example of legal rights can be found in the creation of the **Constitution** of the United States of America, which was written in 1787. The Constitution acts as a rulebook for US citizens and lists their rights under the law. Figure **A** shows two rights included in the American Constitution.

Figure A

> US citizens are entitled to the right to freedom of religion, speech, assembly and petition.
>
> *Amendment One of the US Constitution*

> US citizens have the right to bear arms.
> (US citizens have the right to own a gun to protect themselves.)
>
> *Amendment Two of the US Constitution*

Although these two rights were written in the 18th century, they are still an important part of the constitution and the lives of ordinary Americans today.

Citizens in Britain also have a number of rights. Figure **B** lists some important rights in Scotland.

Figure B

Rights in Scotland

As a citizen you have the right to...

▼

From birth
- Get your own passport (with parental consent)
- Have a bank or building society account
- Have your ears or nose or other body parts pierced

▼

At age 5
- See a U or PG certificate film unaccompanied

▼

At age 12
- See a 12 certificate film
- Buy a pet animal
- Have your opinions listened to on your own adoption

▼

At age 14
- Enter a pub (but you cannot buy alcohol there)
- Ride a horse on a road without head-gear
- Drive an electricity-assisted pedal cycle
- Be employed part-time (with some restrictions)

▼

At age 15
- See a 15 certificate film

At age 16

- Record a change of name officially, without parents' consent
- Drive a moped or invalid carriage
- Leave school
- Get a National Insurance number
- Work full-time if you have left school
- Get married
- Have sex (with someone who is also 16 or over)
- Choose a doctor
- Buy cigarettes and tobacco
- Buy a lottery ticket
- Drink wine or beer with a meal

At age 17

- Drive most vehicles
- Donate blood
- See your birth records if you are adopted

At age 18

- Vote
- Get a passport without parental consent
- Serve on a jury
- Get a tattoo
- Buy alcohol
- Work behind a bar
- Buy fireworks

At age 21

- Drive any vehicle
- Be a candidate in European, parliamentary and local elections

What are responsibilities?

In countries that have certain legal rights there are usually **responsibilities** that go with them. Most of the rights that are held by citizens in Scotland also have responsibilities. For example, in Figure **B** an important right is to drive a car at the age of 17. The responsibility that goes with this right is to ensure that the car is driven safely and that traffic laws are not broken (e.g. the speed limit).

In the Constitution of the USA, all Americans have the right to carry a gun. A responsibility that goes with this right is to ensure that the gun is not used to commit a crime.

SUMMARY

Citizens in Britain have legal rights.

Each right has a corresponding responsibility.

The number of legal rights we have increases from birth to the age of 21.

ACTIVITIES

1 What is a *legal right*?

2 Describe two rights given to US citizens in the US Constitution.

3 What is a *responsibility*?

4 'US citizens have the right to carry a gun.' What responsibility do US citizens have along with this right?

5 What responsibilities match the following rights? Copy and complete the table in your notebook.

Right	Responsibility
To protest	
To drive a car at age 17	
To buy alcohol	
To buy fireworks at age 18	

3.2 What are human rights?

You already know that people living in Scotland have many different legal rights. These rights are guaranteed under the law. However, in many parts of the world there are countries where basic rights simply do not exist.

To solve this problem the **United Nations** (UN) has agreed a list of human rights. Nearly every country in the world is a member of the UN. **Human rights** are rights to which every human being should be entitled. The UN **Universal Declaration of Human Rights** (UDHR) was written in 1948. It provides a framework of human rights for everyone in every country of the world. According to the UDHR, nobody should be made to live without these basic rights.

The UDHR was written after the Second World War, when countries were determined not to have a repeat of the human atrocities carried out during the war. For example, the Holocaust, in which millions of Jews were killed, was then fresh in people's minds. Figure **A** describes some of the main rights contained within the UDHR.

Figure A

Selected rights from the UN Universal Declaration of Human Rights

Article 1	All human beings are born free and equal.
Article 3	Everyone has the right to life, liberty and security.
Article 4	No one shall be held in slavery.
Article 5	No one shall be subjected to torture or cruel, inhuman or degrading punishment or treatment.
Article 10	Everyone is entitled to a fair trial.
Article 13	Everyone has the right to freedom of movement within a country and everyone has the right to leave any country.
Article 17	Everyone has the right to own property.
Article 19	Everyone has the right to free speech.

▲ The United Nations flag.

Convention on the Rights of the Child (CRC), 1989

In 1989 the United Nations produced the **Convention on the Rights of the Child** (CRC). The CRC states the basic human rights that children of the world should have. A child is classified by the CRC as every person under the age of 18.

There are a number of reasons why the UN produced a separate list of rights for the world's children:

■ Children require special safeguards to protect their rights because of their youth and lack of experience. In other words, it is more difficult for children to protect themselves than it is for adults.

■ Some children do not have adults who can look after them and ensure that their rights are protected. There are many children like this across the world.

Figure describes some of the main rights contained in the CRC.

Figure

Selected rights from the UN Convention on the Rights of the Child (CRC)

▲ According to the CRC, every child has certain rights.

Article 2	The child should be protected against all forms of discrimination on the basis of, for example, their sex, religion, and race.
Article 6	Every child has the right to life.
Article 7	Every child has the right to a name and a nationality.
Article 9	A child should not be separated from their parents against their will.
Article 13	Every child should have the right to free speech.
Article 24	Every child should have the right to a high standard of health.
Article 20	A child temporarily or permanently deprived of his or her family environment … shall be entitled to special protection and assistance.
Article 28	Every child should have the right to an education.
Article 32	Every child should be protected from performing work that is hazardous or harmful to their health.
Article 38	No child under the age of 15 should be made to fight in a war.

SUMMARY

Human rights are rights that every human should have.

The United Nations Declaration of Human Rights describes the basic rights that every human being should have.

The United Nations Convention on the Rights of the Child describes the basic rights that every child should have.

These basic human rights do not exist in every country in the world.

ACTIVITIES

1 Why was the United Nations Universal Declaration of Human Rights (UDHR) written?

2 Which Article of the UDHR deals with each of the following areas?
■ *Slavery*
■ *Movement in and out of countries*
■ *Property ownership*
■ *Torture*

3 Why did the UN produce the Convention on the Rights of the Child (CRC)?

4 Select four rights from the CRC that you think are important. Explain why you think they are important.

5 In pairs, make up your own list of rights that you think children should have. How many of these rights are included in the CRC (Figure **B**)?

The UDHR and the CRC are important landmarks in the history of human rights. However, there are many countries in the world where the UDHR and the CRC are simply ignored.

3.3 What is the difference between a democracy and a dictatorship?

What is democracy?

In the United Kingdom it is generally accepted that people have both legal and human rights. The UK is a **democracy**. An important feature of a democracy is that all citizens have rights and responsibilities. However, these are not the only features of a democracy. Study Figure **A**.

Figure A

Features of a democracy

- Government is elected by the people.
- Regular and free elections take place.
- People writing for newspapers, speaking on radio and television, and ordinary people, are able to speak freely. They can criticise the government if they wish.
- All citizens have rights.
- All citizens have responsibilities.

Most countries in the developed world are democracies. The USA, the UK, France, Germany, Japan and Australia are just a few of the countries that can call themselves democracies.

One of the most fundamental rights in a democracy is that everyone over a certain age can vote. In Britain, everyone over the age of 18 can vote in elections. However, this was not always the case. Before 1918, women in Britain were not allowed to vote in **elections**.

A group of women, called **suffragettes**, were important in gaining the vote for women. Emmeline Pankhurst and her followers used both militant and peaceful tactics to get their message across: they wrote letters, organised demonstrations, smashed windows and chained themselves to public buildings.

It was only in 1928, when men and women over the age of 21 could vote, that Britain became a true democracy. It has developed over the years, with rights and responsibilities gradually increasing with the passage of time. Many people think that we should be very protective of our rights because we have not always had them. For example, many argue that everyone who can vote should do so because at one time not everyone in Britain had this right.

▲ The suffragette Emmeline Pankhurst addresses a meeting in Trafalgar Square in 1902.

What is a dictatorship?

A **dictatorship** is the opposite of a democracy. In countries that are dictatorships, people do not have basic rights and responsibilities. In dictatorships, regular and free elections do not take place.

Dictatorships are often ruled by individuals who have seized control of a country and, once in power, have set about maintaining their authority by taking away people's basic rights such as free speech and voting in elections.

▲ A huge street poster of Josef Stalin, which was erected by the Russians in Berlin in 1945.

One of the most famous dictators of the 20th century was Josef Stalin, who was leader of the Soviet Union for more than twenty years. When Stalin became the Soviet Union's leader there were no regular elections and no free speech, and he ordered the killing and torture of millions of people.

Dictatorships and human rights

In countries that are dictatorships, human rights are virtually non-existent. Human rights violations occur throughout the world and not just in dictatorships. Examples of human rights violations include:

■ the use of torture

■ the imprisonment of individuals without trial

■ slavery

■ miscarriages of justice

■ genocide – the mass murder of innocent civilians.

SUMMARY

People have basic rights in a democracy. For example, people have the right to vote for the leaders of a democracy.

People who live under dictatorships do not have basic rights. For example, dictators such as Adolf Hitler deny people the right to vote.

Human rights violations take place in many dictatorships – but also in some democracies.

ACTIVITIES

1 Do you live in a democratic country? How can you tell?

2 What evidence is there that democracies develop over time?

3 Describe the difference between a democracy and a dictatorship.

4 Explain why you think each of the following features of a democracy is important:
   ■ *All citizens have rights.*
   ■ *Governments are elected by the people.*
   ■ *Regular and free elections take place.*
   ■ *The media and ordinary people are free to criticise the government.*

5 Can you think of any dictators who are in power today? Describe, in a couple of paragraphs, why they can be considered a dictator.

6 'Stalin was a fair and just leader of the Soviet Union.' *Communist Party Spokesman*
   Why could the person making this statement be accused of bias?

3.4 What is Britain's record on children's rights?

Why do people criticise Britain's human rights record?

Some campaigners are upset at Britain's record on children's human rights in certain key areas.

Criminal responsibility

Children can be **criminally responsible** for committing a crime in Scotland when they are as young as 8 years old. Some campaigners claim that this is too young. In the rest of Britain the age limit is 10 years. In many countries it is 13 years.

Corporal punishment

In Britain, parents are allowed to use **corporal punishment** to control their children. This usually means smacking. However, some people think that this is a violation of a child's human rights. Corporal punishment in Scottish schools was banned in the 1980s when the practice of belting children ended. However, in 2002 the Scottish Executive dropped its plans to introduce a ban on smacking children under the age of 3.

▲ A Scottish 'belt', which was sometimes used to punish school pupils, until it was banned in the 1980s.

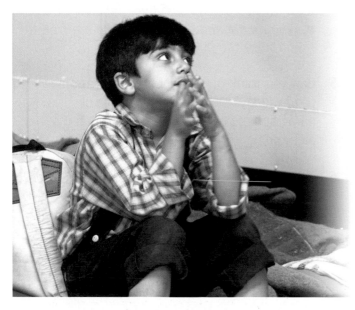

▲ A child asylum seeker – his family hope to be allowed to live in Britain.

Asylum seekers

Asylum seekers believe that they are in grave danger in their own country. They come to Britain for safety because they believe that they will be protected in this country. Asylum seekers and their children are often detained in accommodation whilst a decision is made on their future. Not every asylum seeker is allowed to stay in Britain. Many are sent back to their country. Human rights campaigners are unhappy with the way that some asylum seekers are treated.

Child poverty

Many children in Britain live in **poverty**. This means that they live in families whose income is so low that there is not enough money to live on. Human rights campaigners say the government should do more to improve this situation.

UN report of children's rights in Britain

In October 2002 the UN produced a report, written by the UN Committee on the Rights of the Child, which heavily criticised the British Government's record on children's rights. Read Figure , which describes the main findings of the report.

Figure

From *The Herald*, 5 October 2002

UK DAMNED OVER FAILURE TO BAN SMACKING

United Nations urges repeal of 142-year-old law on chastisement

The United Nations yesterday urged Britain to repeal its 142-year-old law giving parents the right to smack their children.

A pull-no-punches report on Britain's record of protecting its 13.5 million children said it 'deeply regrets' the retention of the defence of 'reasonable chastisement' despite the recommendations of a damning study it published in 1995.

Scotland was tarred with the same brush despite being forced last month to abandon plans to ban smacking.

The UN's report was welcomed by children's charities. Mary Marsh, NSPCC director, said: 'The current law of "reasonable chastisement", devised in the 19th century, is well past its sell-by date. It sends out a dangerous message to parents that hitting children is acceptable and safe, which it clearly is not.

'Children in Germany, Sweden, Denmark and many other countries are protected from being hit by law, why not here too?'

Made up of international experts, the 10-man committee also said it remained concerned that the age of criminal responsibility is 8 in Scotland and 10 in the rest of Britain.

The committee also voiced anxiety that one-third of recruits to the British military each year were below 18, and that the rules allowed them to be deployed in combat.

Concern was also expressed about the high rate of teenage pregnancies in Britain, the number of children suffering mental health problems and the high rate of suicides amongst young people.

However, it was not all bad news for the government, with the committee praising the abolition of corporal punishment in schools and the commitment to end child poverty. The committee, however, said far too many children were still being let down, with poor housing, homelessness, malnutrition, and failures in education among its main concerns.

SUMMARY

Some human rights campaigners question Britain's record on children's rights.

A UN report on the rights of the child in Britain criticised the British Government for their record in a number of key areas.

However, the report did note that Britain had made some progress on the rights of children. For example, corporal punishment in schools has now been outlawed.

ACTIVITIES

1 Read Figure .
  Write a report that describes the main criticisms of the British Government's record on children's rights. Use the following headings in your answer:
  ■ *Corporal punishment*
  ■ *Criminal responsibility*
  ■ *Military service*
  ■ *Poverty*
  ■ *Asylum seekers*

2 Classroom debate:
  'Parents should be allowed to smack their children.'
  ■ *Divide your class into two groups and debate the above statement.*
  ■ *One group should argue in favour of the statement, and one against it.*
  ■ *Appoint an opening and a closing speaker for each group.*
  ■ *The opening speakers begin by putting forward their group's arguments.*
  ■ *After the opening speeches, anyone can put forward their point of view. Any points of view must be put through a chairperson.*
  ■ *At the end of the debate the closing speeches should summarise their group's arguments.*
  ■ *Your class should then vote on whether or not they are in favour of parents being allowed to smack their children.*

3.5 Are children's rights abused abroad?

Children of the world

In some countries the basic human rights of children are violated in a very bad way.

Child soldiers

> No child under the age of 15 should be made to fight in a war. Governments should seek to recruit soldiers who are over the age of 18.
>
> *Convention on the Rights of the Child, Article 38*

Recent estimates suggest that there are almost 300,000 child soldiers throughout the world fighting in over 40 conflicts. In countries such as Burma, Sudan and Afghanistan, children are fighting alongside adults in wars. Many child soldiers are forcibly removed from their homes, taken from their families and made to fight.

Figure Ⓐ

Zaw Tun's Story

> An army recruitment unit arrived at my village and demanded new recruits. Those who could not pay 3000 Kyats had to join the army.
>
> *Zaw Tun, aged 15, ex-army soldier*

Why are children used as soldiers?

An army can exert more control over child soldiers than over adults. Child soldiers also require less food than adult soldiers. Many armies that use child soldiers train them in special camps where they are brainwashed and often given drugs which means they are more likely to follow orders. Modern weapons are very light and can be easily handled by children.

Child workers

> Every child should be protected from performing work which is hazardous or harmful to their health.
>
> *Article 32, Convention on the Rights of the Child*

Throughout the world, children as young as 5 years old are forced to work. The International Labour Organisation estimates that there are 250 million child workers between the ages of 5 and 14.

Children work in areas ranging from farming to factory and construction work. This work is often hazardous. In Asia, for example, many children are forced to work on rug looms (see picture above) which often results in children suffering eye damage and lung disease.

Many children also work as bonded labourers. The families of children involved usually receive money in return for their child undertaking work. This is a form of slavery, and children are often unaware of the debt their families owe to the employers.

Figure

Anwar's Story

Two years ago at the age of 7, Anwar started weaving carpets in a village in Pakistan's province of Sind. He was given some food, but had little free time, and no medical assistance. He was told repeatedly that he could not stop working until he had earned enough money to pay an alleged family debt. He was never told who in his family had borrowed money nor how much they had borrowed. Any time he made an error with his work, he was fined and the debt increased. Once, when his work was considered to be too slow, he was beaten with a stick. Another time, after a particularly painful beating, he tried to run away, only to be apprehended by the local police who forcibly returned him to the carpet looms.

Source: Human Rights Watch

Street children

> A child temporarily or permanently deprived of his or her family environment… shall be entitled to special protection and assistance.
>
> *Convention on the Rights of the Child, Article 20*

Many children in developing countries whose parents have died, or no longer want to look after them, are left to live on the streets.

Street children live in environments where there is no protection or supervision from adults. These children face serious health problems and many are involved in solvent abuse to escape the day-to-day existence they face. For street children, attending school is not possible.

In countries where there are large numbers of street children they are considered a problem to the authorities. Indeed, some reports from Brazil have suggested that many children have been murdered by the police in an attempt to 'cleanse' areas of the problem. This is the worst possible violation of children's human rights.

SUMMARY

Children throughout the world face human rights violations.

Child soldiers are used in many conflicts across the world.

Child workers are often forced to work against their will.

In some countries orphaned children are left to live on the street.

ACTIVITIES

1 How many child soldiers do people think are fighting in wars around the world?

2 If it is OK for governments to make adults fight in a war to protect their country, is it OK for adults to make children fight in a war too? Explain your answer.

3 Read Zaw Tun's story (Figure Ⓐ). Why can what happened to Zaw Tun be described as a human rights violation?

4 Write a short essay on the problems faced by child workers. Use your background knowledge and evidence from Anwar's story (Figure Ⓑ).

5 Imagine that you are a child living on the street. Write a diary extract describing how you feel. Use the following key words:
- *parents*
- *solvent abuse*
- *health problems*
- *education*
- *police*
- *human rights.*

Which groups campaign for human rights?

Human rights organisations

The United Nations (UN) and the **European Union** (EU) campaign to protect human rights. The UN produced the Universal Declaration on Human Rights and the Convention on the Rights of the Child to promote and protect human rights.

▲ The European Union flag.

The EU has produced the European Convention on Human Rights which outlines the basic human rights that people living in the EU should have. It has attempted to end discrimination based on sex, religion, disability or age.

Pressure groups

A **pressure group** is an organisation that is set up to campaign for a specific issue. There are a number of pressure groups that campaign to improve human rights throughout the world. Perhaps the most well-known of these groups is Amnesty International (Figure). Pressure groups involved in human rights campaigns try to put pressure on governments to improve their human rights.

Pressure groups try to influence and work with the UN and the EU to improve human rights. Amnesty International uses a variety of methods to get its message across (Figure Ⓐ).

Figure Ⓐ

Amnesty International

Amnesty International (AI) was set up in 1961 by a British lawyer, Peter Benenson. AI's main aim is to promote human rights across the world and to provide research and action on abuses of human rights. AI opposes human rights abuses such as torture, capital and corporal punishment and the killing of prisoners. AI has over 1 million members and employs people throughout the world. These people meet the victims of human rights abuses and direct campaigns at governments to improve the basic rights of people. AI contacts governments, organises protests and publicises human rights abuses in the media.

In 2001, AI's Campaign Against Torture resulted in some governments making a commitment to pass new laws to prevent the use of torture in their countries.

Despite its attempts, AI reported in 2002 that human rights abuses throughout the world continue. It noted in its Annual Report that in 2001, people in 111 countries reported torture by the police or security forces and that in 54 countries people were arrested without charge or trial.

Read Figure **B**, which is a fictional account of someone whose human rights have been abused.

Figure B

Akan's Story

Akan is a 38-year-old doctor from Zaravia. Zaravia is led by the leader of the country's armed forces. In 1995 Zaravia's dictator banned free speech in newspapers and on radio and television. In 1995 Zaravia's dictator also suspended free elections and made himself 'dictator for life'. In 1996 Akan took part in a street protest against Zaravia's dictator. He was arrested by the police and has been held in prison ever since. Akan still awaits trial. During his time in prison Akan has had several beatings and has been tortured. His family have not seen him since 1997.

SUMMARY

The UN and the EU campaign for human rights.

Pressure groups are also active human rights campaigners.

Amnesty International has a worldwide network of supporters who highlight human rights abuses and attempt to get governments to improve their human rights record.

ACTIVITIES

1 What is a *pressure group*?

2 Describe the main aims of Amnesty International.

3 'The UN and the EU are not concerned with human rights.'
   Do you agree with this statement? Provide evidence to back-up your answer.

4 What methods does Amnesty International use to campaign for human rights?

5 Read Figure **B**. Write a letter to Amnesty International urging them to campaign on Akan's behalf. Include the following in your letter:
   ■ *details of Zaravia's dictatorship*
   ■ *details of why Akan has been imprisoned*
   ■ *details of the human rights abuses Akan has suffered.*

35

4.1 What is representative government?

Democracy

The United Kingdom is a democracy. This means that we, the people, have a say in how the country is run. It is very important that we participate in politics, as this is our direct way of having a say in decisions and laws that are made.

Direct democracy

The birthplace of modern democracy was in Ancient Greece in the city of Athens, over 2,500 years ago. Here it was agreed that all citizens could attend the assembly and vote on all decisions that were taken.

Citizens could also join the government if their name was drawn out of a lottery! In other words, citizens were directly involved in making laws. We call this **direct democracy**.

In a city like Athens it was possible for everyone to have a say because the city was small and government was not complicated. However, just living in Athens did not make you a citizen. Women, slaves and people who didn't own a certain amount of land were not classed as citizens.

▲ A citizen of Ancient Greece, an early democracy.

Representative government

In a country like the United Kingdom, direct democracy would be impossible because there are millions of voters and hundreds of laws made every year. If everyone had a say in which laws would be passed it could take years to pass even a few laws! To solve this problem we elect representatives to speak on our behalf. In this way, a few people can speak for large numbers of citizens and decisions can be made quickly. We call this **representative democracy,** as these representatives make decisions for the people.

Who makes the decisions?

It is very important that we choose the right people to make decisions. To make sure that this happens, the British people take part in elections to elect representatives who will form a **government** and make decisions for them.

By doing this we can participate in our democracy and make sure that our representatives work on our behalf. These representatives are chosen at different levels in British politics to make sure that every citizen is represented.

The people in Figure Ⓐ are some of our representatives in British politics. All of these people make decisions that can affect our lives.

Cathy Jamieson, a Member of the Scottish Parliament (MSP). ▶

Figure

Representatives in British politics

Members of Parliament

Elected to represent people in the House of Commons. **Members of Parliament** (MPs) are elected by the people in a local area known as a **constituency**, and they meet in the House of Commons .This chamber makes decisions and laws which affect every citizen who lives in the United Kingdom. It is here that decisions on things like taxes and defence issues are made.

Members of the European Parliament

Elected to represent people in the European Parliament. Britain has been a member of the European Union since 1973. Members of the European Parliament meet and make decisions that can affect every citizen who lives in the European Union. It deals with economic, social and political issues on a European scale.

Members of the Scottish Parliament

Elected to represent people in the Scottish Parliament. The first Scottish Parliament for nearly 300 years opened in 1999 and the decisions made here affect the lives of people who live in Scotland. In particular, they deal with issues such as health and education.

Councillors

Elected to represent people in the local council. Councillors make decisions which affect a local area. These councils have responsibility for providing services such as refuse collection, schools, parks and libraries.

SUMMARY

We live in a representative democracy.

Elected representatives are chosen to make decisions on our behalf.

There are many different types of representatives in Britain today.

ACTIVITIES

1 Describe what is meant by the term *democracy*.

2 Which ancient city was the birthplace of modern democracy?

3 What do we mean by *direct democracy*?

4 'Direct democracy is an ideal way to run a country.'

   Political party spokesperson

   Do you agree with the view of this political party spokesperson? Explain your answer.

5 Describe what is meant by *representative democracy*.

6 Make a copy of this table. Complete it by adding the four types of representative who meet in these places:

House of Commons	
European Parliament	
Scottish Parliament	
Local council	

How do elections work?

Participation

We are represented in our democracy by a number of elected members. Four important types of representative in the United Kingdom are:

- Members of Parliament
- Members of the Scottish Parliament
- Members of the European Parliament
- councillors.

Participation means taking part or getting involved in an event. Each of the representatives listed above has been chosen after participating in an election. Ordinary citizens can also participate in elections by voting for a candidate. The word *candidate* is the name given to someone who wants to be elected by the voters (*the electorate*).

Who can vote?

In Britain, everyone over the age of 18 can vote, with just a few exceptions. The following groups of people are *not* allowed to vote:

- prisoners
- Members of the House of Lords
- people who are in a psychiatric hospital and are classed as being mentally ill
- visitors to Britain who are not British citizens.

How voting happens

Members of Parliament, or MPs, are representatives who are elected to the House of Commons in London. It is here that the laws which affect every British citizen are made. The process of electing an MP is fairly simple.

Britain is divided into 659 electoral areas, known as **constituencies**. Each constituency is represented by one MP.

Scotland **72**

Northern Ireland **18**

Total seats **659**

England **529**

Wales **40**

Figure Ⓐ Story of a voter on Election Day

1 Tom Isaacs is keen to vote. To make sure that he can place a vote, he visits his local library to check that his name is on the **electoral register**.

2 On the day of the election, Tom visits his local polling station. Tom's polling station is in the local primary school. It is open from 7 am until 10 pm.

At election time, every registered voter, or **constitutent**, has the right to use their vote within their constituency on Election Day. Figure **A** shows how voters participate in Election Day.

Tom has now used his vote. When his polling station closes, all the ballot boxes are removed and sent to a central location where the votes are counted. The count goes on all through the night and often the first results are known by early morning. The candidate with the most votes wins the election and becomes that constituency's representative, or MP.

Other ways of participating in elections

As well as voting, ordinary citizens can participate in elections in a number of ways:

■ **Standing as a candidate**

Anyone over the age of 21 can stand as a candidate in an election. They must pay a deposit, which is returned if they get enough people to vote for them. They must also be nominated by 10 people in the constituency.

■ **Canvassing**

People can canvass on behalf of political parties. This means going around doors asking voters who they intend voting for and trying to persuade them to vote for their own candidate and political party.

■ **Posters, badges and leaflets**

To publicise a candidate, people can put up posters, deliver leaflets and wear badges displaying the name of their preferred party or candidate.

SUMMARY

British citizens can participate in elections by voting and canvassing.

Certain groups in society are not allowed to vote.

We use a specific system when voting.

ACTIVITIES

1 Why did Tom visit the library before Election Day (Figure **A**)?

2 Which of these five people would be allowed to vote in a General Election, and which wouldn't? Explain your answers.
   ■ *Mary Smith, 17 years old and a student at High School*
   ■ *Sanjay Khan, 28 years old, works for a local bank*
   ■ *Mark Litton, 44 years old, lives in Highdon Mental Hospital*
   ■ *Fran Steen, 65 years old and retired*
   ■ *Colin Fort, 52 years old, resides at HM Prison Highleaf*

3 Where are polling stations usually located?

4 Can you explain why polling stations are open for such long hours?

5 Why is it important to carry your polling card with you when you go to the polling station?

6 In what different ways can people participate in elections?

[3] When he arrives, Tom hands his polling card to the polling clerks. You do not have to take your polling card with you, but it saves time if you do. He gives his name and address to the polling clerks along with his polling card, and collects his ballot paper.

POLLING STATION

[4] Tom goes to one of the booths and, using the pencil provided, he marks an X next to his chosen candidate. He has now used his vote.

POLLING BOOTHS

[5] Tom folds the ballot paper and places it in the ballot box next to the polling clerks.

4.3 Why do we vote?

An election victory. ▶

Figure Ⓐ Why vote at all?

Democracy and voting

Britain is a representative democracy. This allows us the chance to have a say in how the country is governed. We are lucky enough to live in a democracy where we are allowed to vote for our leaders. Some people in the world do not have this right. This can happen when people live in a dictatorship. Often the leaders are cruel or harsh and people lead very restricted lives. Can you think of any dictators in the world today? You might even be able to think of some dictators from history.

Using our vote

If we don't like the way in which the country is being run then we can use our vote to show this by voting against the government. Voting does not always have to be concerned with politics. You might have voted for an issue in your local community or in your school. For example, in deciding who should be the class representative, your class probably took a vote or perhaps a show of hands. In this way everyone took part in deciding who should be the representative.

However, there can be problems with voting. The people who win the vote and get the decision they wanted are usually very happy, but some people do not get the result they wanted. Sometimes it is difficult to accept when we do not get what we want in life, but the decision made by the majority has to be respected, even if you personally do not agree with it. You can then campaign to change people's minds in the next election!

But why bother to vote?

Many people do not realise how important our vote actually is. Figure Ⓐ shows the reactions of some citizens when they were asked the question, 'Why should we vote?'

Voting is a waste of time. My vote isn't going to make a difference anyway.

The parties all promise the same things, so why bother?

People have fought and died for our right to vote, so we should always use it.

40

As you can see, not all citizens in a democracy understand why it is important to use our vote. Often, people complain about the work of the government or feel that the government is doing too little, yet they don't even bother to vote!

Well, if we didn't vote then we wouldn't have the right to complain if we disliked government decisions.

The politicians promise so many things but when they gain power they never deliver their promises.

Voting is a democratic right. We should take that right seriously.

m not interested in olitics, so why should I vote?

There are many countries where people don't have the right to vote. We are fortunate to live in a democracy, so we should make use of our vote.

SUMMARY

People should make good use of their vote at election time.

Voting allows us to participate in the way in which our country is run.

People in dictatorships do not have the right to vote freely.

ACTIVITIES

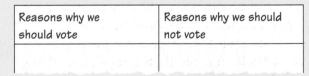

1   Can you give the name of a dictator in the world today?

2   When might you be involved in using a vote?

3   'The fairest way to decide something is the majority decision.'
    Do you agree that the majority decision is the fairest way we have of deciding who runs the country? Explain your thinking.

4   'Why should we vote?'
    Look carefully at the comments made in Figure Ⓐ. Then copy and complete this table:

Reasons why we should vote	Reasons why we should not vote

When you have completed your table, write numbers 1–8 next to the statements, from the one you agree with most (1) to the statement you agree with least (8).

Explain your decision.

4.4 What do political parties stand for?

Right wing and left wing in politics

A **political party** is a group of people who form an organisation with similar political beliefs.

In British politics today, there are many political parties, each with different ideas about how the country should be governed. The two main parties are the Labour Party and the Conservative Party.

Can you think of the names of any other political parties in Britain? The pictures on this page should help you.

But why are there so many parties?

To explain this, we need to understand the meaning of **right wing** and **left wing**.

- **Left wing**

  Parties on the left usually follow some of the following values:

  - strong central government control of the economy – this makes sure that everyone is treated fairly

  - sharing wealth amongst many people

  - equal rights for everyone no matter how wealthy they may be.

- **Right wing**

  Parties on the right usually follow some of the following values:

  - strong control by people with the experience to carry it out

  - little government interference in business unless it is unavoidable

  - strong belief in keeping law and order in the country.

The Labour Party began as a socialist (left wing) party but now, like the other parties, tries to be in the middle. On some issues – like immigration, law and order – the electorate tends to be quite right wing. On other issues – like the National Health Service – the electorate tends to be more left wing. Today, political parties try to match what people will vote for, rather than having strong beliefs, or *ideologies*, that are left or right wing.

Other political parties

Since the end of the First World War in 1918, the Labour and Conservative Parties have been the only two parties to form governments in Britain. For this reason, it is often said that politics in Britain is a 'two-horse race'. However, there are many other parties in Britain that we can vote for. These include regional parties, which generally have policies that favour a certain region of the country.

Liberal Democrats

The Liberal Democrats have campaigned on:

- raising more money through income tax to get more money for education and health

- changing our system of voting.

Scotland

The Scottish Nationalist Party wants Scotland to be an independent country and has had some success in recent elections.

Northern Ireland

There are many different parties in Northern Ireland. The Ulster Unionist Party and the Democratic Unionist Party both want Northern Ireland

◀ Some more unusual candidates appear at election time: here Howling Lord Hope of the Monster Raving Loony Party salutes his supporters.

Kingdom. Sinn Fein and the Social Democratic and Labour Party (SDLP) both want Northern Ireland to be part of a single united Republic of Ireland, totally separate from Great Britain.

Other parties

Other parties involved in British politics today include:

- The Green Party
- Plaid Cymru
- UK Independence Party.

Have you heard of any of these parties? You might want to find out more about them. Ask your teacher, or make use of the school library or internet to discover what these parties stand for. Some useful websites include:

www.labour.org.uk

www.conservatives.com

www.liberaldemocrats.com

SUMMARY

Parties can be described as being right wing or left wing.

There are many different political parties in Britain today.

Parties compile policies which outline what they will carry out if they win the election.

ACTIVITIES

1 Write out the meaning of *political party*.

2 Name the two main political parties in Britain today.

3 Copy and complete this table by listing in the correct column the political values of left wing and right wing politics set out below.

Left wing	Right wing

- Strong belief in keeping law and order in the country
- Strong central government control of the economy – this makes sure that everyone is treated fairly
- Strong control by people with the experience to carry it out
- Equal rights for everyone no matter how wealthy they may be
- Little government interference in business unless it is unavoidable
- Sharing wealth amongst many people

4 'British politics is a two-horse race.' What does this mean?

5 Name the current leaders of the following political parties:
- *Labour Party*
- *Conservative Party*
- *Liberal Democrats.*

6 Regional parties focus on the politics of particular regions. Describe the policies of **one** regional party from either Scotland, Wales or Northern Ireland.

You will need to do some research on your own for this activity.

4.5 Who wins a constituency?

Every constituency in Britain elects a Member of Parliament to represent them in the House of Commons. But how do we decide which candidate wins the constituency?

Constituency results

The electoral system used in the United Kingdom today is called 'first past the post'. This means that the candidate with the most votes wins and becomes MP for that constituency. On pages 38–39 we looked at Tom Isaacs as he prepared to cast his vote in the constituency. Once his vote had been cast and the polling station had closed, his vote and thousands of others were taken to a central location to be counted.

Every candidate's votes are added up and the results recorded. Figure Ⓐ shows the election results for Blackston constituency.

As you can see, the candidate with the most votes in this constituency was Dev Singh. He gained 16,000 votes whilst the 'runner-up' was Edith Simon with 15,000 votes. Dev Singh became MP for Blackston constituency, as with 16,000 he had the largest number of votes. Dev gained 1,000 votes more than Edith. The difference between the number of votes for the winning candidate and those for the candidate who is second, is called the *majority*.

Working out a representative's winning majority is extremely important. The size of the majority gives us an idea of how likely it is that representatives can win at the next election. For example, if Dev Singh had a majority of 1 there is a very good chance that another candidate may win the Blackston constituency at the next election. However, if Dev Singh had a majority of 15,000 it is unlikely that he would lose the next election, unless he did something very wrong or his party became very unpopular.

Figure Ⓐ

Votes in Blackston constituency

Edith Simon	Conservative Party	15,000
Dev Singh	Scottish National Party	16,000
Ian Norris	Labour Party	10,000
Mary Brydon	Liberal Democrats	7,000

Safe seats

A safe seat is a constituency in which candidates from the same party usually win in every election. Representatives who have large majorities of over 3,000 votes are said to have safe seats.

Marginal seats

A marginal seat is a constituency in which candidates from more than one party have a chance of winning. Representatives who have small majorities of less than 3,000 votes are said to have marginal seats.

2001 General Election

Look carefully at Table **B**. These are the actual results for the constituencies of Coatbridge and Chryston, and Castle Point from the 2001 General Election.

Table B

Votes in the 2001 General Election

Coatbridge and Chryston		Castle Point	
T Clarke (Lab)	19,807	R Spink (Cons)	17,738
P Kearney (SNP)	4,493	C Butler (Lab)	16,753
T Tough (Lib Dem)	2,293	B Boulton (Lib Dem)	3,110
P Ross-Taylor (Cons)	2,171	R Hurrell (UK Independent)	1,273
L Sherridan (SSP)	1,547		

◄ Tom Clarke talks to two young voters.

SUMMARY

The British electoral system is known as 'first past the post'.

Constituencies can be described as safe seats and marginal seats.

The majority is the difference between the first and second candidates.

ACTIVITIES

1 What name is given to the British electoral system?

2 Calculate the winning majority in each constituency in Table **B**.

3 Describe the difference between a *safe seat* and a *marginal seat*.

4 Which constituencies in Table **B** are safe seats? Explain your answer.

5 Which constituencies in Table **B** are marginal seats? Explain your answer.

6 'R Spink won the Castle Point constituency by a huge majority.' Do you agree with this statement? Give reasons for your answer.

7 Why is it easier for a representative to hold on to a safe seat?

4.6 How is the government formed?

Government

After a General Election is held, the political party with the most MPs forms the government. Each MP has a seat in the House of Commons, so the number of MPs is often called the number of 'seats'. New governments are elected in Britain every four to five years. The current Labour Government was first formed at the 1997 General Election and also won the 2001 election. In a General Election all 659 constituencies in Britain vote to keep their existing MP or to elect another one. The results of the 659 constituencies are added up and the party with the most seats becomes the government.

Table **A** shows the results of the 2001 General Election.

Table A

Party	Seats
Labour	413
Conservative	166
Liberal Democrats	52
Scottish National Party	5
Others	23
	659

As you can see, the Labour Party had the largest majority of votes in this election. Labour, therefore, became the government after the election.

Prime Minister

The leader of the party that wins the General Election becomes the **Prime Minister**. The Prime Minister's responsibility is to run the government. It is the role of government to make the day-to-day decisions which enable the country to run smoothly. This involves dealing with areas such as Health, Education, Defence and Transport. Can you think of any other areas that governments deal with?

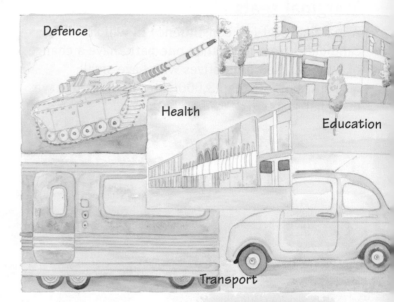

Tony Blair became the British Prime Minister for the second time after the Labour Party won the 2001 General Election. This was the first Labour Government in Britain for 18 years. The party in government before Tony Blair was the Conservative Party, led by John Major.

Tony Blair became the British Prime Minister in 2001. ▶

Cabinet

As Prime Minister, one of Tony Blair's most important jobs is to appoint a Cabinet. **Cabinet** is the name given to the group of MPs who run the major government departments. Cabinet usually consists of around 20–25 individuals who are known as **Government Ministers** (Secretaries of State). Table **B** identifies some Cabinet posts and describes what the job entails:

Table B

Cabinet post	Description of role
Prime Minister	Leader of the Government
Deputy Prime Minister	Deputy Leader of the Government
Chancellor of the Exchequer	Responsible for the economy
Foreign Secretary	Deals with foreign affairs
Home Secretary	Looks after affairs in Britain
Health Secretary	Responsible for health

Each Cabinet minister usually has responsibility for running one of the major government departments. For example, the Health Secretary has overall responsibility for running the National Health Service (NHS) in England and in Wales. This job also involves devising new policies which are intended to make the NHS better in England and Wales.

The individual people who hold these posts can change quickly! Try to find a current list of Cabinet posts. A likely website for finding these posts is:

www.parliament.uk or www.cabinet-office.gov.uk

SUMMARY

Governments are elected at least every five years in Britain.

The leader of the winning party becomes Prime Minister.

Cabinet runs the major government departments.

ACTIVITIES

1 After a General Election, which party forms the government?

2 How often are General Elections held?

3 Which party won the 2001 General Election?

4 Calculate the Labour Government's majority in the 2001 General Election.

5 'The result of the 2001 General Election was very unfair on all of the other parties. Between them the other parties gained more seats than the Labour Party.'
Do you agree with this statement? Provide evidence to support your answer.

6 Who becomes Prime Minister after a General Election?

7 Name the current Prime Minister.

8 How many individuals usually make up Cabinet?

9 What are some of the responsibilities of the Secretaries of State?

◀ The UK Cabinet in session.

What is Parliament?

Perhaps you have heard politicians discussing issues on television or you may have even been to London to see Big Ben. Have you ever wondered how the government makes important decisions? These activities take place in the Houses of Parliament. **Parliament** is the name given to the part of the British political system that deals with law making. It is the most important part of the British political system. Many people tend to think of Parliament as just the House of Commons. However, Parliament is much more than that. It is made up of the **House of Commons,** the **House of Lords** and the **Monarch** (the Queen).

Figure Ⓐ

The structure of Parliament

The House of Commons is where the elected Members of Parliament (MPs) take part in debates and vote on different issues to do with running the country. It is here that the government makes laws that affect all of us.

How is the House of Commons organised?

MPs are members of the House of Commons. After a General Election, the political party with the most MPs in the House of Commons forms the government. Because Britain has a long history, the House of Commons has many traditions. This means there are certain ways of doing things in the House of Commons, and the MPs must follow these rules and traditions. One of the most obvious traditions is in the way in which the seating is organised. Figure Ⓑ shows how the House of Commons is organised.

Figure Ⓑ

The House of Commons

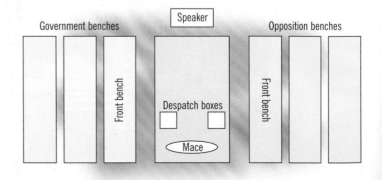

The layout of the House of Commons is very important. The government (winning party) sits on one side and the opposition parties sit across from them. The **opposition** is all the political parties that are not in government. Separating the government benches from the opposition benches are two **despatch boxes** and the **Mace**. The Mace is an ornate pole which is a symbol of the House of Commons and is used for ceremonial purposes.

The Prime Minister and the other ministers from the winning party sit on the **front benches** in the Commons. The opposition also has promoted MPs on their front benches and they are called the **Shadow Cabinet**. The rest of the MPs sit in the back benches on the same side of the House as their political party, behind those on the front benches. This is where the majority of MPs in the House of Commons sit and they are therefore called **backbenchers**.

When you see the House of Commons in action you will notice a great deal of debating going on. It is the role of the **Speaker** to keep order in the House of Commons – and he or she often has a difficult job keeping MPs in line!

▲ The Speaker in the House of Commons.

SUMMARY

Parliament is divided into the House of Commons and the House of Lords.

In the House of Commons, MPs sit in certain areas.

The House of Commons works to support or oppose the government.

Work of the House of Commons

The House of Commons works to support or oppose the government; it passes **bills**, examines the work of the government, and represents the constituents. This is done in many ways. The most obvious way is by debating. When you see the House of Commons in action you will notice that it often involves MPs standing and discussing issues. We call this **debate**. Other work involves **Committee** meetings, asking the Prime Minister questions at **Prime Minister's Question Time** and asking government ministers questions during **Question Time**.

ACTIVITIES

1 Copy and complete the following:

> **Parliament**
>
> House of   House of   Monarchy
> C_____   L_____   (Queen)

2 In what part of Parliament do MPs belong?

3 Draw a diagram to show the layout of the House of Commons.

4 Where do ministers sit in the House of Commons?

5 Why are the majority of MPs called *backbenchers*?

6 Who makes up the *opposition*?

7 Name the person who keeps order in the House of Commons.

8 Give examples of the work of the House of Commons.

9 'The House of Commons is the most important part of Parliament.'
   Do you agree with this statement? Give reasons for your answer.

4.8 How does Parliament make laws?

Law making

The main job of Parliament is to pass laws. In a democracy it is very important that the government listens to the people by passing laws that the people want.

The ideas for new laws come from many different groups. They might come from the **manifesto** of a political party. They could be in response to pressure from the public, e.g. as a result of **lobbying** by a pressure group or government department, or Cabinet could put them forward.

The ideas for a new law are called *bills*. Often ideas for new laws come from the government, usually from members of Cabinet.

Cabinet has a very important role in law making. The members of the Prime Minister's cabinet are very senior ministers in the government and their opinion is important to the Prime Minister.

The role of the House of Commons

Before a bill can become a law it has to be debated in the House of Commons. This gives MPs the chance to discuss issues or raise any complaints that they might have. In this way we can say that we have a democracy in Britain, as our representatives have a say in decisions that are made. For some bills, particularly those that are very controversial, a great deal of debate takes place – and this can result in the House of Commons being a very noisy place!

You might want to look at some debates that have taken place in the House of Commons. A useful website might be:

www.parliament.uk/commons

A debate in the House of Commons. ▶

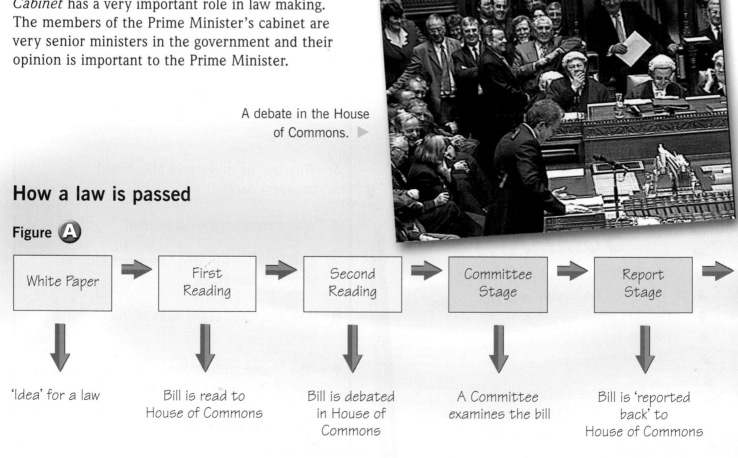

How a law is passed

Figure Ⓐ

White Paper	→	First Reading	→	Second Reading	→	Committee Stage	→	Report Stage	→
↓		↓		↓		↓		↓	
'Idea' for a law		Bill is read to House of Commons		Bill is debated in House of Commons		A Committee examines the bill		Bill is 'reported back' to House of Commons	

Once the bill has been debated by MPs in the House of Commons it is then looked at by groups of MPs in Committees. These MPs have a lot more time to look at the bill in detail. If they think that the bill needs changes made to it then this is done at this stage. The bill is then debated again in the House of Commons.

Once the bill has been debated it is passed to the House of Lords. Finally it is passed to the Queen for **Royal Assent**. This means that the queen agrees with the bill. Another tradition in Parliament is that the Queen never refuses to sign a bill.

▼ A debate in the House of Lords.

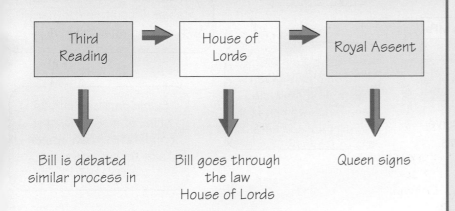

| Third Reading | → | House of Lords | → | Royal Assent |

Bill is debated similar process in

Bill goes through the law House of Lords

Queen signs

As you can see, there are many different stages in passing a law in Britain. It is very important that the government passes laws that meet the needs of people in our country today.

SUMMARY

The main role of Parliament is in making laws.

There are many different stages for a bill to become a law.

The House of Commons is very traditional and the procedures for voting are very unusual.

ACTIVITIES

1 What is the main role of Parliament?

2 Name two groups that might put forward an idea for a new law.

3 What is a *bill*?

4 (a) Copy Figure Ⓐ into your notebook.
   (b) In your own words, describe how a bill becomes law.

5 'Laws are rushed through Parliament. I don't believe that that our MPs think carefully enough about them.'
   Marcus McIntosh

   Can Marcus be accused of exaggeration? Explain your answer.

6 Why does the Queen never refuse to sign a bill?

7 The House of Commons passes many new laws every year. You might want to gather newspaper articles which discuss laws that are going through the Houses of Parliament.

4.9 What kind of people become MPs?

Society is made up of many groups of very different people. We think of Britain as being a **multicultural society** made up of people from different races and religions. However, when asked to think of MPs in the House of Commons, many people think of a stereotype (see page 12). People tend to think that all MPs are white and male. This stereotype is not that far from the truth. Women account for only 18% of the MPs in the House of Commons. Women, however, are not the only group who are under-represented in the House of Commons. Blacks and Asians are also under-represented there. But why is this the case?

Women in the House of Commons

In 2002 there were 659 MPs in Britain. Given that women make up over half of the population of Britain you would expect that roughly half the MPs in the country would be women – about 300–330 MPs. Yet this is not the case. Look at Table Ⓐ.

Table Ⓐ

Women MPs in the House of Commons

	Women candidates	Number of women MPs
1992	568	60
1997	information not available	120
2001	information not available	118

In the 1997 General Election there was a massive change in the number of women MPs. This was because the Labour Party actively promotes women through **positive discrimination**, to ensure that more women are chosen as parliamentary candidates.

Why are women under-represented in the House of Commons?

Anne Brown is very keen to become involved in politics. However, she is very aware that women find it difficult to become MPs. In Figure Ⓑ she is considering some of the difficulties that women face.

Figure Ⓑ

Many women are often still expected to look after children, to cook and to do housework – even if they have a full-time job during the day. This means that many women do not have time to join a political party.

The House of Commons does not provide childcare facilities, so many women find it difficult to arrange childcare.

Family commitments mean that working in London can be very difficult for some women.

Parliament meets at strange hours, often going on until late in the evening. This can cause difficulties for many women with children.

The House of Commons is often seen as a male club and many women feel intimidated there.

Some parties tend to think of men as better candidates than women and so put more men forward.

Ethnic minorities in the House of Commons

Ethnic minorities make up about 6% of the population of Britain. You might therefore expect that roughly 6% of the MPs in Britain would be from ethnic minorities. However, just as for women, this is not the case.

Ethnic minorities are also under-represented in Parliament. In 1997, Britain's first Muslim MP, Mohammed Sarwar, was elected in the Glasgow Govan constituency, and in 2001 two more MPs from an Asian background joined the House of Commons. However, people from ethnic minorities still made up a small percentage – 1.4% – of the total number of MPs in the House of Commons in 1997. It is not good to have certain groups under-represented in Parliament. Parliament makes the laws for Britain, and the groups that are under-represented often feel left out when decisions are being made. Ethnic minorities can be victims of **racism** in Britain – being discriminated against when it comes to jobs, housing and education. If Blacks and Asians are not represented properly in Parliament then laws might not be passed to help fight prejudice and discrimination.

Why are ethnic minorities under-represented in the House of Commons?

■ Black and Asian people often find it difficult to get selected to stand as a candidate by the local constituency party.

■ Local political parties are often not keen to have candidates from ethnic minorities as they feel that they will not win many votes.

■ Like women, some ethnic minorities see the House of Commons as a white male club and may feel intimidated by it.

◄ Mohammed Sarwar, the MP for Glasgow Govan.

SUMMARY

Women and ethnic groups are under-represented in the House of Commons.

Many women face prejudice from voters.

Some ethnic minorities face the problem of racism when they consider standing for election.

ACTIVITIES

1 Name two groups of people that are under-represented in the House of Commons.

2 Look at Table **A**.
'There was a huge drop in the number of female MPs between 1997 and 2001.'
Martin McHugh
Why might Martin be accused of exaggeration? Provide arguments to back-up your answer.

3 Describe what the Labour Party is doing to try to increase the number of women Labour MPs.

4 Look carefully at Figure **B**. Why might some women find it difficult to become an MP?

5 Give a reason to explain why there are few Black and Asian MPs.

6 'There has been some progress made in recent years in the number of Asian MPs.'
Alison Paterson
Do you agree with Alison's statement? Give reasons for your answer.

4.10 What does an MP do?

The work of an MP

Elections for MPs are held approximately every five years and, once elected, MPs sit in the House of Commons in Parliament, in London. MPs have two main jobs:

- the work they do *outside* Parliament
- the work they do *inside* Parliament.

Outside Parliament

Outside Parliament an MP's main job is to represent their constituents (the people who live in an MP's constituency). Constituents go to their MP with their problems. They can contact their MP in three main ways:

- They can write letters to their MP.
- They can visit their MP at his/her surgery. A surgery is usually held every Saturday morning when the MP is back home from Parliament. People can go along and discuss problems with their MP at the surgery.
- They can go and meet their MP at Parliament. If an issue is very important, a number of constituents might go to meet their MP at Parliament, e.g. if a local factory is going to shut down. This is known as *lobbying* your MP.

▲ An MP deals with letters from her constituents.

Inside Parliament

MPs can work on behalf of their constituents inside Parliament. However, they are usually also involved in other types of work within Parliament. They can be involved in debate in the House of Commons, be a member of a committee or committees, ask questions at Question Time, propose Private Members' Bills, work for their political party, or involve themselves with the work of the government (e.g. as a government minister).

What sort of problems do people take to their MPs?

Different sorts of problems are taken to an MP by their constituents. For example:

- Unemployed people who do not get enough money from the Department for Work and Pensions (DWP)
- People who have been charged too much income tax
- People who have problems with a government organisation
- People who are annoyed about a new prison being built near their house.

What action can MPs take to help their constituents?

The most common action taken by an MP is to write a letter on behalf of the constituent:

■ to the local council

■ to a government minister

■ to a private company.

An MP has far more influence than an ordinary member of the public and has more chance of having action taken.

And remember, MPs have to represent all members of the constituency – even those who did not vote for them!

An MP's work is very varied and can involve working long hours. Look carefully at Susan Wong MP's diary in Figure Ⓐ.

Figure Ⓐ

Diary of an MP

8 am	Answer constituents' mail
9 am	Committee on Health Reforms
11.30 am	Attend debate in House on local factory closure
1 pm	Working lunch with trade union leader from constituency
2.30 pm	Take party of pupils from local school on a tour of Commons
4 pm	Meeting with the Chief Whip
6 pm	Back to London flat for quick dinner
7 pm	Attend debate on government's new Education Bill
10.30 pm	Leave House of Commons and head back home

Of course every day might not be as busy as Susan's but, as you can see, MPs are involved in many different jobs.

SUMMARY

MPs are involved in work in Parliament.

MPs are involved in work in their constituency.

People ask their MP to deal with lots of different problems.

MPs use different methods when dealing with constituents' problems.

ACTIVITIES

1 What is an MP's main job *outside* Parliament?

2 Describe an MP's main job *inside* Parliament.

3 Describe the three main ways in which constituents can contact their MP.

4 Write down some examples of problems that constituents take to their MP.

5 Name the most common action taken by MPs to help their constituents.

6 Why do MPs have more chance of getting action taken than ordinary members of the public?

7 What would an MP do if a constituent came to him/her with a problem and the constituent had not voted for the MP in the last election? Explain your answer.

8 Find out the name of your local MP. Look in your local newspaper or visit your local library to find this information.

4.11 What are the roles of the House of Lords and the Monarchy?

The House of Commons is involved in very important stages in passing bills in Parliament. But Parliament also includes the House of Lords and the Monarchy. What role does each of these play in our democracy?

The role of the House of Lords

You have looked at the stages a bill goes through. Once the bill has gone through the House of Commons it is passed to the House of Lords. The House of Lords is often called the *Second Chamber*. What is meant by the House of Lords?

Bob and Angela have been working on the role of Parliament in their Modern Studies class, but Bob is confused by the topic 'The House of Lords'. In Figure Ⓐ, Angela describes the role of the House of Lords to Bob.

The House of Lords spends a great deal of its time debating issues. In this way the House of Lords keeps a check on the work of the House of Commons. Many people argue that this is very necessary. Can you think of a reason why this would be useful in a democracy?

The role of the Monarch

Once a bill has gone through all of the stages in the House of Commons and House of Lords, it is passed to the Queen. This is called *Royal Assent*. When a bill has gone through all of these stages it becomes an **Act**, the proper name for a law. Just like the House of Lords, many people argue that the monarchy is not needed in the United Kingdom. They say it is old-fashioned and a waste of money.

Figure Ⓐ

I'm confused, Angela. What exactly is the House of Lords?

Well, the House of Lords is a bit like the House of Commons but the people who sit there have not been voted there by the electorate.

But surely in a democracy we should elect our representatives?

Yes, you're right, but Britain has a long history and the House of Lords has always been a part of Parliament. Over the years the power of the House of Lords has been reduced but it still plays a very important role in our democracy.

Okay. So what does it do?

Its main role is to carry out tasks which the House of Commons doesn't have the time to do. They often debate items more fully than the House of Commons because they're not so busy. It also acts as a second voice in case the House of Commons becomes too powerful.

That's right. In this way we can make sure that the House of Commons doesn't get too powerful and always works on behalf of the people.

In other words, it keeps an eye on the House of Commons?

Look carefully at Figure .

Figure B

The Royal family is a waste of time. They cost the taxpayers a lot of money and do nothing for the people.

I believe that this country benefits from having a Monarchy. The Royals are loved by many people and they bring millions of pounds into Britain every year from tourists. The Queen is also respected across the world.

As you can see, there are many arguments *for* and *against* the Monarchy. In future it might even be a topic for heated debate in the House of Commons!

Reforming the House of Lords

Many people say that we do not need a House of Lords. They say that it is undemocratic because its members are not elected by the people and, as a result, there have been many calls for changes to be made to the House of Lords.

A recent example of a controversial bill was the White Paper (bill) on the Reform of the House of Lords. Many people have claimed that the House of Lords is old-fashioned, outdated and unnecessary. Many members of the House of Lords did not agree with this bill to make it more modern, and the result was that the government faced a great deal of criticism when it was introduced to Parliament.

You might like to find out more information on recent bills in the Houses of Parliament. To do this, you could visit a website such as:

www.parliament.uk.

The work of Parliament

In recent years Parliament has been involved in making laws on many different issues. Most of these are passed easily because they are not controversial. This means that, although laws might concern us, for many people they do not hold much interest. Other laws, however, might cause a great outcry from the public or from the within the House itself.

SUMMARY

The House of Lords and the Monarchy play an important role in law making.

Many people argue that the House of Lords is outdated.

Many people claim that the Monarchy is no longer necessary.

ACTIVITIES

1 Carefully read the conversation in Figure **A**. For each of the following statements answer *true* or *false*:
   (a) The members of the House of Lords are elected representatives.
   (b) Recently, the power of the House of Lords has decreased.
   (c) One of the main roles of the House of Lords is to debate issues.
   (d) The House of Lords is not interested in the work of the House of Commons.

2 'The House of Lords and the Monarchy are necessary parts of our democracy.'
   Copy and complete the following table by providing arguments *for* and *against* the House of Lords and the Monarchy.

	Arguments for	Arguments against
House of Lords		
Monarchy		

3 As a class, debate the motion:
   'This House believes that the House of Lords is outdated.'
   Divide the class into two groups. Each side should now prepare arguments *for* and *against* this motion. You could set out the class in the same style as the House of Commons (see page 48). Now see which side can debate more strongly for their side of the argument.

5.1 Different people, different needs?

Meeting needs

Britain today is made up of many different people. We live in a society where people are very different. Look around you. There are many people living in your town, village or even your street, and everyone is different. In Britain today there are people who are young, people who are old, people who follow different religions, have different ethnic backgrounds, jobs, standards of education and wealth.

All of these people have different **needs**. For example, you will have very different needs from those of your elderly neighbour. Your younger sister may have different needs from you in the local community. Government, however, has the responsibility of trying to meet the needs of *everyone* in society. With demands from so many people and so many needs, it is very difficult to please everyone. The government has to decide which needs have to be met, and how to meet these needs.

Here are some of the needs that have to be met in our society:

- health needs
- educational needs
- financial needs
- mobility needs.

Look carefully at Figure A.
What needs does each person have?

Figure A

As you can see, there are different people with different needs in our society. How does the government try to meet some of these needs?

National government meeting needs

Governments have to try to meet many of these needs. They do this on a national level by looking after the many different interests that the nation has. For example:

- The government has to look after the *defence needs* of the nation. If we go to war with another country then it is the government's responsibility to ensure that we are prepared for war. This means that we should have a properly trained and equipped army, and that it should have sufficient weapons to defend the nation.

Monique   Nadir   Jane   Ben

Jane is 81 years old. She has a problem getting up and down the stairs in her house. She is hoping to get a stairlift installed in her home.

Nadir has done very well in his Standard Grade exams. He hopes to do well in his Higher exams next year.

Ben has worked for his local steel company for 27 years. Unfortunately the company is soon to close. He doesn't know when he will find a new job.

Monique fell off her bike and hurt her wrist. Her mum insists that she visits the local hospital to have it examined by a doctor.

- People in this country also have different *welfare needs*. In Britain today we have a welfare state. This means that the government takes responsibility for people's welfare by providing for us in times of need.

- Many people have *financial needs*. To meet these needs the government provides benefits such as the Jobseekers' Allowance to help people when they are out of work, and pensions to assist the elderly when they retire.

These are just a few examples of the ways in which the government meets the needs of people.

Local councils meeting needs

But it is not just the government that meets people's needs. Our local councils also meet our needs by providing local services such as libraries, swimming pools and public parks. They are also responsible for areas such as housing, social services and refuse collection.

Scottish Parliament meeting needs

The Scottish Parliament meets the needs of Scottish people by providing for our needs in society. It meets our *health needs* by providing us with healthcare. To do this it has responsibility for the National Health Service in Scotland, which provides us with doctors and nurses, hospitals and clinics. Many people have a need to be provided with an *education*. To do this the Parliament funds education at many different levels. This can range from primary education, to university education for students who follow degree courses.

European Parliament meeting needs

The European Parliament meets our needs in many different ways. For example, it provides the European Court of Justice which helps us if we feel that our legal rights are not being met by our legal system. It also ensures that manufacturers make toys and electrical equipment which meet tough safety standards.

There are many more needs in society. Can you think of any others?

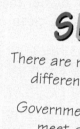

SUMMARY

There are many different people with different needs in our society.

Government departments help to meet some of these needs.

Voluntary organisations such as charities also help to meet people's needs.

ACTIVITIES

1 Look carefully at Figure **A**. Match up the needs with the people:
- *Health needs*   Jane
- *Educational needs*   Monique
- *Financial needs*   Nadir
- *Mobility needs*   Ben

2 Describe how the national government meets the following needs:
- *defence needs*
- *welfare needs*
- *financial needs*.

3 What do local councils provide to meet our needs?

4 In what two ways does the Scottish Parliament meet our needs?

5 In what ways does the European Parliament meet our needs?

6 'Now that I'm a pensioner, the government makes no attempt to meet my needs.'
John Marcetti, aged 72 years

Do you agree with John's statement? Give reasons for your answer.

What is local government?

Here we look at local government: at what it means, how it works in practice, and what its role is in a democracy.

How did local government begin?

Local councils play a very important role in the lives of citizens both in Scotland and in the rest of Britain. They developed in the 19th century in response to the massive public health and housing problems that existed at that time. With the government based in London, there were no local organisations to deal with people's problems. Glasgow Corporation was one of the first of these local councils – it provided the city with clean water, which helped to stop the spread of a disease called cholera. Gradually, organisations became involved in other local issues. Education, housing and public health were particularly important areas to these early councils.

Throughout the 20th century the role of local councils expanded and they now provide a wide range of services to communities. In 1996 the number and names of local councils changed. In Scotland we now have a system of local government that involves 32 local authorities (Diagram **A**).

Diagram A

Local authorities in Scotland

What is the role of local government?

Obviously the government based in London cannot be expected to organise individual towns, so it is the role of the local council to deliver many of our key services. Figure **B** lists some of the services provided by a typical council.

Many other services are provided and these include areas such as social services, police and fire services, and planning.

1 Orkney	12 Stirling	23 West Dunbartonshire
2 Shetland	13 Argyll and Bute	24 East Dunbartonshire
3 Western Isles	14 North Ayrshire	25 North Lanarkshire
4 Highland	15 South Ayrshire	26 Glasgow City
5 Moray	16 East Ayrshire	27 East Renfrewshire
6 Aberdeenshire	17 South Lanarkshire	28 Renfrewshire
7 Aberdeen City	18 Scottish Borders	29 Inverclyde
8 Perth and Kinross	19 East Lothian	30 Clackmannanshire
9 Angus	20 Midlothian	31 Falkirk
10 Dundee City	21 City of Edinburgh	32 West Lothian
11 Fife	22 Dumfries and Galloway	

▲ A library run by the local government.

Figure **B**

Housing Dealing with rented council housing is often a large part of a council's work. The council provides, repairs and improves council housing within the local authority area.
Education Nursery, primary and secondary schools educate all the children in the local authority area.
Roads To keep roads safe, the council maintains and repairs them. It is also responsible for street lighting and car parks, and for gritting roads during winter.
Recreation services This is a huge area and covers services such as cemeteries, parks and swimming pools, and encourages tourism in the area.
Environmental protection The council is responsible for environmental health, collection and disposal of refuse (waste), as well as consumer protection and public health.
Cultural services This department looks after libraries and museums and provides a range of cultural events such as concerts and theatrical productions.

How does local government work?

Local councillors are directly elected in local elections and they are responsible to people for the quality of services that the council provides. Local council elections take place in Scotland every four years. Can you find out when the last local election was? Another group of people who hold responsibility in local councils are *council officials*. Unlike councillors, these posts are paid and their job is to be responsible for the day-to-day running of services within the authority. An example of a council official is the Director of Education or the Chief Executive.

Council meetings

All local councillors get together regularly at meetings of the full council. It is here that important decisions are made about the council's services. Smaller groups of councillors also meet on council committees, and here they discuss and make decisions on particular services. For example, current education decisions relating to the organisation of schools within an authority area may be discussed at a meeting of the Education Committee.

SUMMARY

Local councils provide services at a local level.

There are many different departments in the local council.

Council officials run services for the local council.

ACTIVITIES

1 How many local authorities are there in Scotland today?

2 Why are councils essential in the local community?

3 Name three council departments and describe the role of each one.

4 Name two groups of people who work for the council on our behalf.

5 Where are many decisions about council services made?

6 'Local councils do nothing for the people in my community.'
Why might this person be accused of exaggeration?

7 *Investigating local government*
Find out the name of your local council and then collect information relating to its work. You may wish to look in local newspapers or visit your school library.

5.3 How do councils meet people's needs?

Needs in the local community

Within our local communities, many people have different needs, which have to be met. People might have health needs – for example, an elderly person may need to be cared for around the clock. Young people have a need to be educated. Others may need assistance in keeping their gardens tidy. Through council departments, local councils attempt to meet these needs by providing many different services.

Look carefully at the case studies in Figure . Each of these people makes use of council services.

Figure

 **Laura Munro** is 10 years old and attends her local primary school, Glencairn Primary School. Laura lives 3 miles away, so every morning she arrives at school by bus. Here she meets her friends and, as today is Monday, the girls are busy discussing when they will meet tonight to go swimming at their local pool.

 **Alice Campbell**, 74, lives in a sheltered housing complex. Sheltered housing provides elderly people with round-the-clock care. Every weekday she goes to her lunch club, which is held in the local community centre, and here she meets up with friends for a chat and a cup of tea.

 **Joyce Chan** owns a house on the Glencairn estate. She and her husband have decided to add an extension to their home to give each of their children their own bedroom. To do this, Joyce has to get planning permission and so she has applied to the local council for this.

As you can see, each of these people receives help from their local council. Can you think of any other ways in which we make use of our local council?

How are council services funded?

It costs a lot of money to provide local government services. They are funded in four main ways (Diagram **B**).

■ **The government** provides some of the money.

■ **Council charges,** such as entrance fees for swimming pools or rents from council housing, are another way of bringing in funds.

■ **Council taxes** and **rates** provide further funding. The amount of money that people pay in council tax is based on the value of their house.

Diagram **B**

Local government funding, 1998–99 (gross income)

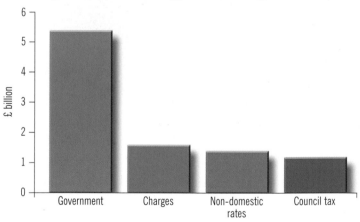

 **Bob Smith** retired from his job with the social services department of the local council five years ago. Since then his health has deteriorated but, with the help of the local council, he is able to stay in his own home. A home help comes round every day to help with Bob's housework and, since he is no longer fit, the council grass-cutting scheme has been a great help.

▲ Local councils are responsible for running schools in their area.

However, in recent years many councils have found that they still do not have enough money to carry out essential repairs. One particular problem for councils has been in paying for the upkeep of schools.

What is PPP?

As a result of a lack of money, the government has encouraged councils to become involved in **Public Private Partnership** (PPP) programmes. This means that councils use private firms to design, build and operate public buildings such as schools. This money is then paid back over a set time-period. Glasgow City and Falkirk Councils use PPP to build state-of-the-art schools in their areas, for example. However, some schools have had to be closed under the scheme and many people, especially in trade unions, do not agree with this system of funding. The government and local councils have faced much criticism for using PPP. Despite this criticism, however, many councils are now using PPP to make improvements to schools.

Your local council may be considering using PPP to make improvements to your own school. Have a look in the local press and watch out for local news bulletins on television to gather information on the subject.

SUMMARY

Councils meet people's needs in many different ways.

Councils are funded from different sources.

Recent funding initiatives such as PPP have met a great deal of criticism.

ACTIVITIES

1   Copy and complete the table below. State which council department (or departments) meets the needs of each person.

	Council department
Laura Munro	
Alice Campbell	
Joyce Chan	
Bob Smith	

2   Look carefully at Diagram **B**.
    'Councils receive most of their funding from council tax payments.'

    Terry Ahmed

    Why can Terry be accused of exaggeration? Give reasons for your answer.

3   What is meant by *PPP*?

4   'PPP is an excellent way of funding improvements to our schools.'

    Council spokesperson

    Can the council spokesperson be accused of bias? Explain your answer.

5.4 How do councillors meet our needs?

Representatives in Britain

There are many representatives in Britain today who work to meet our needs in society. Members of Parliament, Members of the Scottish Parliament, Members of the European Parliament and councillors all work to meet our needs. We take a look here at how councillors represent us.

What does a councillor do?

At a local level, many people in the local community have needs, and these have to be met. The most likely person to speak on your behalf is your local councillor.

Councillors are chosen by us at elections to run local services on our behalf. These elections are called local elections.

The map on page 60 shows the local authorities (councils) that comprise Scottish local government. See if you can find the authority in which you live.

Councillors are elected to their positions at local government elections which take place every four years. The electoral system is similar to the one used in national elections, when Members of Parliament are elected (see pages 38–39). Councillors have the power to make decisions that affect our everyday lives in the local community. They are also responsible for workers who deliver services within the local council area, such as teachers, housing officers, social workers and refuse collectors.

Unlike MPs, councillors are not paid, although they receive an allowance of approximately £4,000 a year, plus allowances for travelling expenses when they are carrying out council business.

Needs of people in the local community

Often we may find ourselves having to deal with a problem at local level that is difficult to solve. These needs have to be met. Figure Ⓐ shows some examples of the needs of people in the local community.

Figure Ⓐ

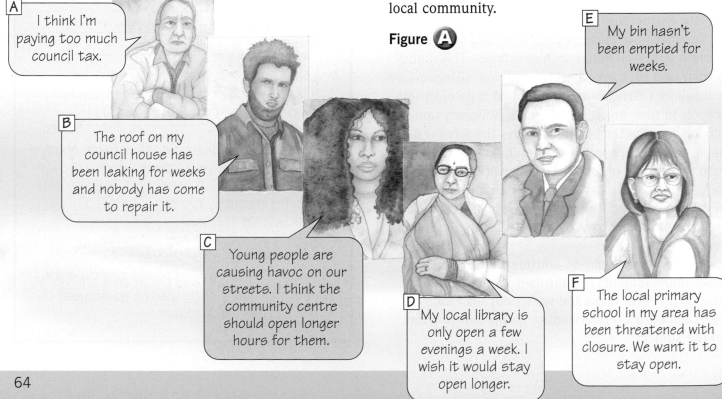

A — I think I'm paying too much council tax.

B — The roof on my council house has been leaking for weeks and nobody has come to repair it.

C — Young people are causing havoc on our streets. I think the community centre should open longer hours for them.

D — My local library is only open a few evenings a week. I wish it would stay open longer.

E — My bin hasn't been emptied for weeks.

F — The local primary school in my area has been threatened with closure. We want it to stay open.

When our needs relate to local problems, then we call upon our councillor to represent us. Through the work of the local council, councillors can make direct contact with council departments on our behalf.

Councillors are usually local people. This means they live in the local community that they serve, and are well-known in the local community. As well as doing their official council work, they may find themselves meeting people in the streets and holding 'unofficial' surgeries at the local shopping centre.

Many people argue that the role of the councillor is an essential part of democracy. Few people actually see their MP, as much of an MP's work takes place in London, and they may live outside their constituency. Councillors, though, are able to meet the needs of people more directly, because they are local, and know their own community well.

A local councillor meets some of the people in the community that he represents. ▼

SUMMARY

Councillors are chosen in local elections to represent people in the local community.

Local councils offer a wide variety of services.

Councillors are well placed to meet the needs of local people.

ACTIVITIES

1   Name four different types of representative in Britain today.

2   Which of these representatives meets our needs in the local community?

3   (a) In which local authority do you live?
    (b) Find out the name of your local councillor. You might like to visit a website such as www.cosla.gov.uk to discover this information.

4   Compare the role of an MP and a councillor. Give one *similarity* and one *difference* between them.

5   Look carefully at the statements of local people in Figure Ⓐ. Copy and complete the table below by writing the letter of each problem beside the correct council department. The first one has been done for you.

Council department	Statement
Refuse collection	E
Council housing	
Libraries	
Education	
Council tax	
Recreation facilities	

6   'Councillors are useless in dealing with local problems.'
    Do you agree with this statement? Give reasons for your answer.

5.5 How did Scotland shape its identity?

In 1999 Scotland got its first Parliament in nearly 300 years. Before we look in detail at how the Scottish Parliament operates and meets the needs of the Scottish people, it is necessary to understand why the Scottish Parliament was created. To do so we must first consider some of the historical events that have been important in shaping Scotland to give it the **identity** we know today.

Auld enemies

For many years Scotland's history has been linked to the fortunes of its English neighbours. In the past the fate of Scotland as a nation has often been decided as a result of bloody battles with its old enemy – England.

As early as the 13th century there was strong evidence that Scotland's relationship with England could be fraught with tension. The death of the great Scottish king, Alexander III, in 1286 resulted in a chain of events that led to the English king Edward I (the 'Hammer of the Scots') invading Scotland in 1296 and controlling its land and people for a number of years.

During the 20 years of the Scottish Wars of Independence from 1296, a number of Scottish heroes emerged and some have assumed legendary status in Scotland. The names of William Wallace, popularised in the Mel Gibson movie *Braveheart*, and King Robert the Bruce, have helped to create a distinct Scottish identity. Indeed, it was Bruce's victory over the English at the Battle of Bannockburn in 1314 that guaranteed Scottish **independence** for almost 400 years.

In 1603 Scotland's relationship with England became closer when the Crowns of Scotland and England were united under the leadership of King James VI of Scotland (James I of England). The Union of the Crowns meant that the same person ruled Scotland and England, although they both remained independent nations.

In 1707 Scotland and England were effectively united into a single country – Great Britain. The Act of Union of 1707 meant that the Scottish Parliament no longer passed laws. Laws were now to be made by the British Parliament based in London, and Scotland lost its independence.

Apart from Bonnie Prince Charlie's failed attempt to seize control of the British throne in 1745–46, Scotland and England have lived in peace since the Act of Union of 1707.

Scottish football fans ▶

A distinct Scottish identity

Scotland lost its independence in 1707 – and not all Scots were happy with this situation. However, a number of distinct features of Scottish life have helped the country to retain a sense of identity and nationhood.

Culture

Scotland has held on to its own unique cultural identity. It has long had its own writers, poets and special forms of music that help to create a Scottish identity. Indeed, Scotland has its own language, Gaelic, which is still spoken in parts of the country today. Scotland also has its own national daily newspapers which have a distinctly Scottish flavour. For many, the greatest expression of a distinct Scottish identity can be found in the strong following of the national football team.

Education

After 1707 Scotland developed its own education system, which has always remained quite separate from the system in England. Today, pupils in Scotland sit Standard Grade, Intermediate and Higher courses, while their English counterparts sit GCSEs and A-Levels.

▲ Robert Burns, 18th-century Scottish poet.

Legal system

The Scottish legal system is also significantly different from the system of laws used in England, Wales and Northern Ireland. Scottish lawyers are specifically trained to practise law in the Scottish courts. A good example of how the law differs in Scotland is the existence of the Children's Hearing System, which has a key role to play in the supervision and welfare of Scottish children. The Children's Hearing System does not exist in England.

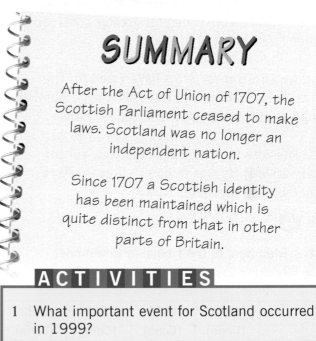

SUMMARY

After the Act of Union of 1707, the Scottish Parliament ceased to make laws. Scotland was no longer an independent nation.

Since 1707 a Scottish identity has been maintained which is quite distinct from that in other parts of Britain.

ACTIVITIES

1 What important event for Scotland occurred in 1999?

2 Match the list of dates below with the correct event

1286	Union of the Crowns
1296	Death of Alexander III
1314	Failed attempt by Prince Charles to seize the British Crown.
1603	Act of Union results in Scotland losing its independence
1707	Edward I invades Scotland
1745–46	Victory at Bannockburn restores Scottish independence

3 Describe the main features of Scottish culture which help to create a distinct Scottish identity.

4 What evidence is there that the Scottish educational and legal systems are quite distinct from those in the rest of Britain?

Why do we have a Scottish Parliament?

Throughout the 20th century a growing number of Scots became unhappy that laws affecting Scotland were being made in the House of Commons in London. These Scots called for greater control over decisions that affected Scotland.

Since the 1960s most Scots have voted for the Labour Party. However, in the 1980s large numbers of English people voted for the Conservatives.

Few Scots voted for the Conservatives, yet the Conservative Party was in power from 1979 to 1997. Table Ⓐ illustrates this.

Table Ⓐ

Scottish Members of the House of Commons, 1979–97

	1979 (Cons)	1983 (Cons)	1987 (Cons)	1992 (Cons)
Labour	44	41	50	49
Conservative	22	21	10	11
Liberal	3	8	9	9
Scottish National Party	2	2	3	3

(Party winning General Election in brackets)
This meant that many more Scots said they didn't like Scotland being run from London. There were two main points of view on this in Scotland by the early 1980s: those who wanted independence, and those who wanted devolution.

The main supporters of independence were the Scottish National Party (SNP), which was formed in 1934 to campaign for an independent Scotland. The SNP still campaigns today for Scotland to break away from the rest of Britain and to be an independent country.

Other people wanted Scots to have a greater say in making their own laws, but at the same time believed that Scotland should remain part of the United Kingdom. These people believed in **devolution**. Devolution simply involves giving Scotland greater control over making its own laws within the UK. One way of achieving devolution, its supporters argued, would be to create a Scottish Parliament.

The 1997 Devolution Referendum

After the Labour Party won the 1997 General Election it began to fulfil one of its most important election promises: the creation of a Scottish Parliament – in other words, devolution.

In September 1997 the New Labour Government organised a **referendum** to find out if the people of Scotland wanted a Scottish Parliament or not. A referendum is an organised vote on a single issue. The devolution referendum asked Scots two simple questions:

■ Should there be a Scottish Parliament?
■ Should any new Scottish Parliament be able to vary the rate of tax?

For each of these questions voters were asked to respond by putting a cross in either a YES or NO box on a ballot paper.

Not all of the major parties in Scotland campaigned for devolution. Whilst Labour, the Liberal Democrats and the Scottish Nationalists urged Scots to vote

'YES YES', the Conservatives were against the creation of a Scottish Parliament. The Conservatives feared that devolution would eventually lead to Scottish independence and the break-up of the United Kingdom. This is called a **Unionist** viewpoint.

The results of the referendum were conclusive. Over half of those who voted were in favour of a Scottish Parliament and that it should be able to vary the rate of tax. Diagram **B** shows the referendum results.

Diagram **B**

Scottish Devolution Referendum Results, 1997

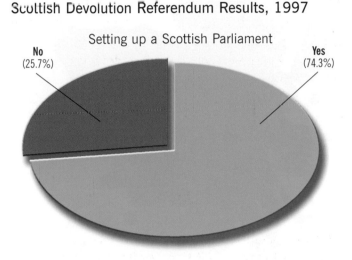

Setting up a Scottish Parliament
No (25.7%)   Yes (74.3%)

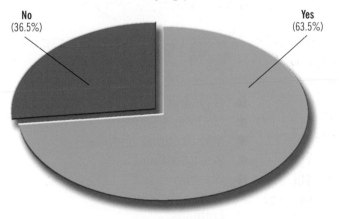

Tax varying powers
No (36.5%)   Yes (63.5%)

Elections to the new Scottish Parliament were arranged to take place in May 1999.

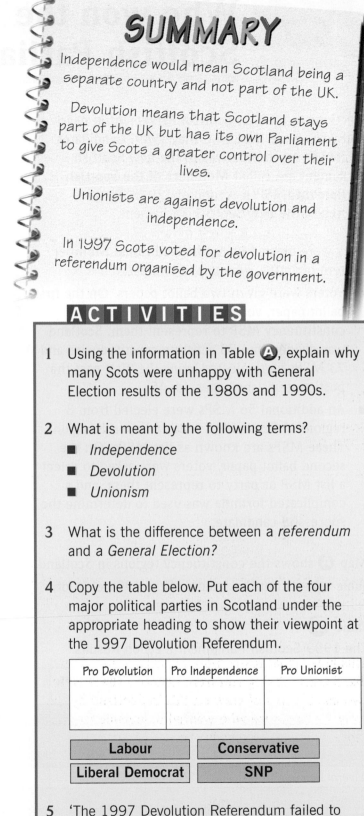

SUMMARY

Independence would mean Scotland being a separate country and not part of the UK.

Devolution means that Scotland stays part of the UK but has its own Parliament to give Scots a greater control over their lives.

Unionists are against devolution and independence.

In 1997 Scots voted for devolution in a referendum organised by the government.

ACTIVITIES

1 Using the information in Table **A**, explain why many Scots were unhappy with General Election results of the 1980s and 1990s.

2 What is meant by the following terms?
■ *Independence*
■ *Devolution*
■ *Unionism*

3 What is the difference between a *referendum* and a *General Election?*

4 Copy the table below. Put each of the four major political parties in Scotland under the appropriate heading to show their viewpoint at the 1997 Devolution Referendum.

Pro Devolution	Pro Independence	Pro Unionist

Labour   **Conservative**
Liberal Democrat   **SNP**

5 'The 1997 Devolution Referendum failed to produce a clear result.'
Using the information in Diagram **B**, explain why this statement is an exaggeration.

Who won the 1999 and 2003 Scottish Parliament elections?

Elections to the first Scottish Parliament in nearly 300 years were held on 6 May 1999. Candidates elected as representatives to the new Scottish Parliament are called **Members of the Scottish Parliament** (MSPs). A total of 129 MSPs were elected to the new Scottish Parliament.

They were elected using the **Additional Member System** of voting, which is in two parts.

- Voters were given two ballot papers. On the first ballot paper, voters were asked to select a constituency MSP to represent them. Scotland was divided into 73 separate constituencies and 73 MSPs were elected using the 'first past the post' system (see pages 44–45).

- An additional 56 MSPs were elected from 8 regions in Scotland (7 MSPs from each region). These MSPs are known as **list MSPs**. On the second ballot paper, voters were asked to select a list MSP or party to represent them, and a complicated formula was used to determine the successful candidate.

Map **A** shows the constituency regions in Scotland. Table **B** sets out the results of the 1999 election.

Map **A**

Scottish parliamentary regions

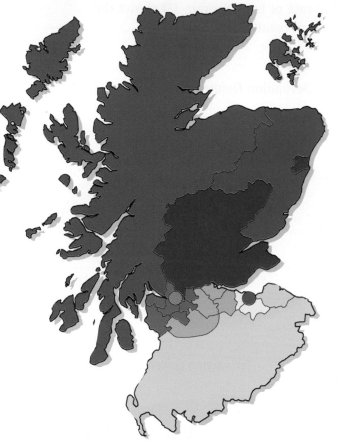

- Highland and Islands
- Northeast Scotland
- Mid-Scotland and Fife
- West Scotland
- Glasgow
- Central Scotland
- Lothians
- South Scotland

Table **B**

The 1999 Scottish Parliament Election Results

Party	Constituency MSPs	Regional list MSPs	Total MSPs
Labour	53	3	56
SNP	7	28	35
Conservative	0	18	18
Liberal Democrat	12	5	17
Green	0	1	1
Scottish Socialist	0	1	1
Independent	1	0	1
TOTAL	73	56	129

Table C   The 2003 Scottish Parliament election results

Party	Constituency MSPs	Regional list MSPs	Total MSPs
Labour	46	4	50
SNP	9	18	27
Conservative	3	15	18
Liberal Democrat	13	4	17
Green	0	7	7
Scottish Socialist	0	6	6
Independent	2	1	3
Scottish Senior Citizen's Unity	0	1	1
TOTAL	73	56	129

Labour won the Scottish Parliament election in 1999 with a total of 56 MSPs – but it did not have more than half of the total MSPs (65). In other words, Labour did not have a **majority,** so it was unable to pass laws in the new Scottish Parliament without significant opposition from the other parties.

In order to have complete control of the Scottish Parliament, the Labour Leader, Donald Dewar, entered into a partnership with Jim Wallace, Leader of the Liberal Democrat Party. With Labour's 56 seats, and the Liberal Democrats' 17, the two parties had 73 seats – more than half of the total. Together they could pass laws more easily in Parliament because they had a majority.

When two or more parties agree to work like this together in government, it is called a **coalition** government.

The 1999 election results are also interesting because two small parties, the Green Party and the Scottish Socialist Party, each won one seat in the Scottish Parliament. It is unlikely that small parties like these would ever be able to gain enough votes to take a seat in the House of Commons.

2003 Scottish Parliament Elections

After the 2003 elections, Labour and the Liberal Democrats continued to govern Scotland in a coalition government. However, the coalition's majority was cut. The 2003 results were significant due to the important gains made by smaller parties such as the Greens and the Scottish Socialists.

SUMMARY

A total of 129 MSPs are elected to the Scottish Parliament using the Additional Member System.

Labour won the 1999 Scottish Parliament election but did not achieve a clear majority.

This led Labour and the Liberal Democrats to share power in a coalition government.

ACTIVITIES

1   What is the name given to elected representatives of the Scottish Parliament?

2   Study Table **B** carefully.
   (a) Which party won the 1999 Scottish Parliament election?
   (b) Did this party have a clear majority? Explain your answer.

3   What is meant by the term *coalition government*?

4   Explain why the Labour Party had to enter into a coalition government with the Liberal Democrats in 1999 and 2003.

5   'The Scottish Parliament election results of 2003 were significant because of the performance of smaller parties.' Explain this statement.

6   Write a 250-word report which describes the main differences in party support between 1999 and 2003. Consider each party's performance in your answer.

5.8 What are the Scottish Parliament and Scottish Executive?

As Scottish citizens it is important that we understand how both the Scottish Parliament and the Scottish Government are organised.

The Scottish Parliament

Powers

The Scottish Parliament was given the power to create new laws and to change or abolish laws in some areas. At the same time the British Parliament kept its power over certain areas. The main areas over which the Scottish and British Parliaments each have responsibility are shown in Table **A**.

Table **A**

Powers of the Scottish and British Parliaments

Scottish Parliament	British Parliament
Agriculture, Fishing and Forestry	Defence
Economic Development and Transport	Economic Policy
Education	Employment
Environment	Foreign Policy
Health Social	Security
Law and Home Affairs	
Local Government, Social Services and Housing	
Sport and the Arts	

Clearly, the Scottish Parliament has control over most of the areas affecting the day-to-day lives of Scots.

Layout

The Scottish Parliament is arranged in a semicircle. This is in significant contrast to the House of Commons, where MPs face each other in rows of benches (see page 48). Some argue that the arrangement of the Scottish Parliament encourages less heated and more constructive debates than the 'adversarial' debates of the British Parliament.

▲ The Scottish Parliament in session.

Meetings

The Scottish Parliament works much shorter hours than the House of Commons. MSPs attend the Scottish Parliament during normal office hours. Some argue that this has encouraged more women to become MSPs – in 1999, 37% of MSPs were women compared with only 18% in the House of Commons.

The Presiding Officer

The Presiding Officer of the Scottish Parliament performs a similar role to that of the Speaker in the House of Commons. The Presiding Officer is an MSP who is elected by all 129 MSPs. The Presiding Officer acts as a referee or chairperson during full meetings of the Parliament, and is responsible for making sure that Parliament's rules are not broken. David Steel was elected as the Scottish Parliament's first Presiding Officer in 1999. Unlike the Speaker of the House of Commons, the Presiding Officer does not wear any special ceremonial wig and gown.

The Scottish Executive

The Scottish Executive is the name given to the government of Scotland. The Scottish Executive consists of MSPs from the Scottish Parliament. The party with a majority in the Scottish Parliament elections forms the Scottish Executive. No party achieved a majority in 1999, so the Scottish Executive was a coalition government with power shared between the Labour and Liberal Democrat Parties.

Table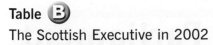
The Scottish Executive in 2002

SCOTTISH EXECUTIVE

First Minister	Jack McConnell (Labour)
Deputy First Minister and Minister for Justice	Jim Wallace (Liberal Democrat)
Minister for Education and Young People	Cathy Jamieson (Labour)
Minister for Enterprise, Transport and Lifelong Learning	Ian Gray (Labour)
Minister for the Environment and Rural Development	Ross Finnie (Liberal Democrat)
Minister for Tourism, Culture and Sport	Mike Watson (Labour)
Minister for Social Justice	Margaret Curran (Labour)
Minister for Finance and Public Services	Andy Kerr (Labour)
Minister for Health and Community Care	Malcolm Chisholm (Labour)
Minister for Parliamentary Business	Patricia Ferguson (Labour)

The First Minister

The First Minister is like a Prime Minister for Scotland. The First Minister is chosen by the Parliament's MSPs and has overall control over the Scottish Executive. He or she appoints other Ministers to the Scottish Executive – see Table **B**. Each Minister has responsibility for a Scottish Executive Department.

ACTIVITIES

1 Describe the role of the Presiding Officer.

2 What is the name given to the Government of Scotland?

3 Which party (or parties) forms the Scottish Executive after an election?

4 Describe the role of the First Minister.

5 Look at Table **B**.
Which Ministers would deal with each of the following problems?
- *The building of new hospitals in Scotland*
- *A strike by teachers*
- *A proposal to build a new rail link from Glasgow to Glasgow Airport*
- *Scotland's bid to host the 2008 European Nations Football Championships*
- *An outbreak of foot and mouth disease in livestock*

SUMMARY

The Scottish Parliament has its own distinct powers. The chamber is in the form of a semicircle. Meetings of the Scottish Parliament are controlled by the Presiding Officer.

Meetings of the Scottish Parliament take place during office hours. A notable feature of the new Scottish Parliament is the high number of women MSPs.

The Scottish Executive is the name given to the government of Scotland. The head of the Scottish Executive is the First Minister.

6 Copy and complete the following table. Use your knowledge of the House of Commons to help you.

Differences between the Scottish Parliament and the House of Commons

	Scottish Parliament	House of Commons
Location	Edinburgh	
Name of representative		MP
Number of representatives		
Hours worked		
% women representatives		

7 Use the internet to discover the names of current Scottish Executive Ministers. A useful website is:

www.scottish.parliament.uk

5.9 How does the Scottish Parliament meet people's needs?

The role of MSPs

MSPs perform a vital role in Scotland. The work they do both outside and inside the Scottish Parliament helps to meet the needs of Scottish people.

MSPs outside the Scottish Parliament

MSPs do a lot of work outside the Scottish Parliament. Like MPs, MSPs hold regular surgeries, which give their constituents an opportunity to discuss any problems they are experiencing. People bring problems to their MSP because they know that they are very influential. They may raise constituents' problems in the Scottish Parliament or contact members of the Scottish Executive on their behalf.

MSPs inside the Scottish Parliament

MSPs play a crucial role in the Scottish Parliament in attempting to meet the needs of Scottish people. They do this in several ways.

Voting

MSPs take part in the Scottish Parliament by voting for or against new laws which are proposed, usually by the Scottish Executive. In this way MSPs have a say in the creation of laws that are designed to protect and help people in Scotland.

Committee work

MSPs can join a number of committees in the Scottish Parliament. Diagram Ⓐ shows the main committees that were set up in 1999.

▲ First Minister Jack McConnell.

As you can see, there is a committee for each subject or policy area. Each committee consists of between 5 and 15 MSPs, whose job is to examine any new laws proposed by the Scottish Executive that are relevant to their committee. For example, if the Scottish Executive propose a new law in relation to Scottish education, the Education, Culture and Sport Committee would examine the proposals carefully.

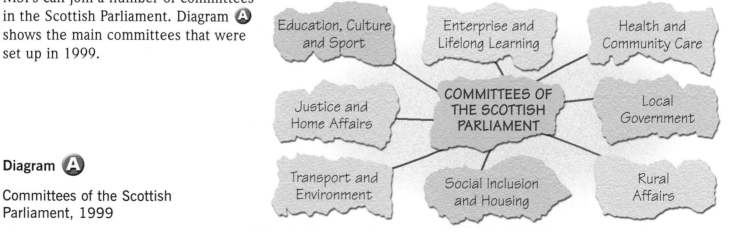

Diagram Ⓐ

Committees of the Scottish Parliament, 1999

Education, Culture and Sport

Enterprise and Lifelong Learning

Health and Community Care

Justice and Home Affairs

COMMITTEES OF THE SCOTTISH PARLIAMENT

Local Government

Transport and Environment

Social Inclusion and Housing

Rural Affairs

Questions

MSPs can ask oral and written questions in the Scottish Parliament, which a member of the Scottish Executive must answer. The First Minister holds a weekly Question Time when he is quizzed by MSPs. For example, if a factory is to close with the loss of many jobs, the MSP for the constituency in which the factory is located, could ask the First Minister how he intends to deal with the situation.

Private bills

An individual MSP can propose a new law in the form of a **Private Bill**. Private Bills are often concerned with moral issues, such as the Private Bill proposed by Labour MSP Mike Watson which was successful in banning foxhunting in Scotland.

Debates

MSPs can take part in debates in the Scottish Parliament. This gives them the opportunity to speak out on behalf of their constituents.

The Scottish Parliament, 1999–2003

The Scottish Parliament has passed numerous laws since 1999. Some of them have been highly controversial. Three of these are described here.

Student tuition fees

Universities usually charge their students tuition fees. Until 1997 these tuition fees were paid by the British Government. However, when Labour came to power in 1997, it decided to make students pay for their own tuition fees. Many MSPs were unhappy with this situation and they put pressure on the Scottish Executive to think again. In January 2000 the Scottish Parliament voted not to make students pay their own tuition fees – the Scottish Executive will pay them. Many argue that this is a good example of the new Parliament meeting the needs of students.

Ban on foxhunting

In February 2002 the Scottish Parliament passed a law which banned foxhunting in Scotland. This law was introduced by the Scottish Parliament before it was passed by the British Parliament.

Care of the elderly

In 2002 the Scottish Parliament passed a law which provided for free personal care of the elderly in nursing and residential homes in Scotland. This policy has not been introduced in the rest of the UK.

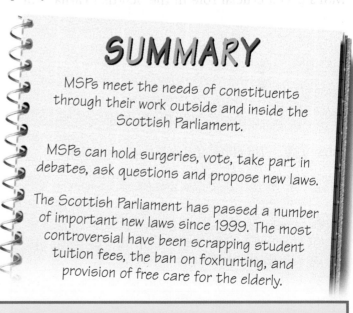

SUMMARY

MSPs meet the needs of constituents through their work outside and inside the Scottish Parliament.

MSPs can hold surgeries, vote, take part in debates, ask questions and propose new laws.

The Scottish Parliament has passed a number of important new laws since 1999. The most controversial have been scrapping student tuition fees, the ban on foxhunting, and provision of free care for the elderly.

ACTIVITIES

1   Describe the main method of contacting an MSP in their constituency.

2   Write a report which describes the role of an MSP inside the Scottish Parliament. Use the following headings:
    - Voting
    - Committee Work
    - Questions.
    - Private Bills
    - Debates

3   'The Scottish Parliament has achieved nothing since 1999.'

    Describe the evidence which supports the view that the above statement is an exaggeration.

5.10 What is the European Union?

At the end of the Second World War, the countries of Europe decided that they should find a way of making sure they never went to war again. Belgium, France, Germany, Italy, Luxembourg and the Netherlands signed agreements on trade and industry. By 1973, Denmark, Ireland and the United Kingdom had also become members of the organisation known as the **European Economic Community** (EEC). This organisation was so successful that by 1995 it had 15 members, and its name was changed to the **European Union** (EU), as we know it today.

What does the EU do?

The EU is an international organisation, which looks after the social, political and economic needs of its members. It is also involved with non-member nations in its aid, economic and defence programmes. Diagram **C** outlines the work of the EU.

Table A   The European Union in 2003

EU member states:	Thirteen countries are currently involved in the enlargement process:
Austria	Estonia, Latvia, Lithuania, Poland,
Belgium	Czech Republic, Slovakia, Hungary,
Denmark	Slovenia, Romania, Bulgaria, Malta,
Finland	Cyprus and Turkey.
France	All of these countries are destined to
Germany	join the EU, once they have fullfilled the
Greece	criteria for membership. With twelve of
Ireland	them (the ten countries of Central and
Italy	Eastern Europe, plus the islands of
Luxembourg	Cyprus and Malta) the EU has opened
Netherlands	negotiations for membership.
Portugal	Negotiations with Turkey cannot begin
Spain	until that country meets the political
Sweden	criteria for membership.
UK	

Table B   Timeline of the European Union

1952	The European Coal and Steel Community (ECSC) is founded
1958	European Economic Community (EEC) begins: Belgium, France, Germany, Italy, Luxembourg and the Netherlands join the EEC
1973	Denmark, Ireland and the UK join the EEC
1981	Greece joins the EEC
1986	Spain and Portugal join the EEC
1992/93	The Single Market, The Maastricht Treaty, name changed to the European Union (EU)
1995	Austria, Finland and Sweden join the EU
	The Amsterdam Treaty is signed
2003	Many former Eastern European countries apply for membership

Diagram C

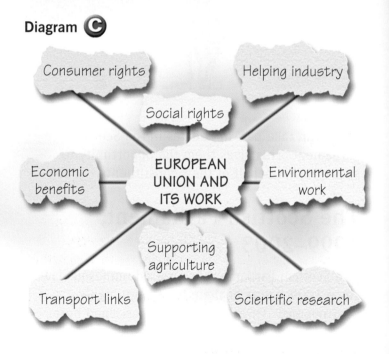

- Consumer rights
- Helping industry
- Social rights
- Economic benefits
- EUROPEAN UNION AND ITS WORK
- Environmental work
- Supporting agriculture
- Transport links
- Scientific research

How are decisions made?

There are four main institutions in the EU: the European Parliament, the Council of Ministers, the Commission, and the European Court of Justice. We look here at the work of the European Parliament in more detail.

The European Parliament

Just like the Parliaments of the United Kingdom and Scotland, the European Parliament is a *directly elected* assembly. It has representatives from across the member countries of the EU, known as **Members of the European Parliament** (MEPs). Just like our Scottish Parliament, the European Parliament meets to discuss issues that are of interest to member countries. In total, there 626 MEPs (Table **D**). Do you know the name of your local MEP? A likely website to help you find out this information is: www.europa.eu.int

Table D   MEPs per country

Austria	21	Italy	87
Belgium	25	Luxembourg	6
Denmark	16	Netherlands	31
Finland	16	Portugal	25
France	87	Spain	64
Germany	99	Sweden	22
Greece	25	United Kingdom	87
Ireland	15		

Issues in the EU

Enlargement

An important issue for the EU today is **enlargement**. Because the EU has been so successful, many other countries are keen to join. However, some of the member nations do not wish to see the EU expand because they fear that it will become too large. Recently, former Eastern European countries such as Poland have applied for membership, and some of these countries are likely to become members in the near future.

The single currency

In January 2002 many member countries agreed to change to the single currency, known as the **Euro**. This currency has replaced individual countries' currencies and we now use this money when we travel to Europe. For example, if you take a holiday in Spain this year you will use the Euro instead of pesetas. Britain has not changed to the Euro but it may do so in the future.

Social issues

One of the main roles of the EU is to make sure that member nations have similar **living standards.** The EU introduced the **Social Chapter.** This means that the EU carries out many initiatives to improve the living and working conditions of its members.

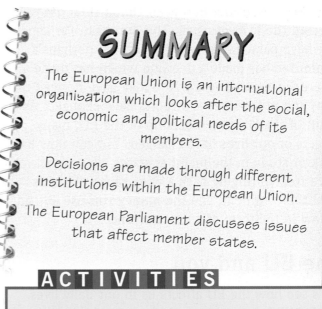

SUMMARY

The European Union is an international organisation which looks after the social, economic and political needs of its members.

Decisions are made through different institutions within the European Union.

The European Parliament discusses issues that affect member states.

ACTIVITIES

1   Copy and complete this timeline table to show membership of the EU:

Year	Members
1958	
1973	
1981	
1986	
1992	

2   What needs does the EU look after?

3   Using Diagram **C**, state some of the issues dealt with by the EU.

4   Where do EU representatives meet?

5   Look carefully at Table **D**.
    (a) Which country has the largest number of MEPs in the European Parliament?
    (b) Which country has the smallest number of MEPs in the European Parliament?

6   Describe three issues in the EU today.

How does the European Union affect our lives?

Perhaps you don't even realise it, but being a member state of the European Union (EU) has affected the lives of us all. The European Parliament may have passed Acts which affect us, perhaps a committee has made a decision which has made a difference to our lives, or you may have noticed that signs and procedures at airports have changed. As a result of the UK's membership of the EU, many aspects of our lives have changed. You can now live, work or study in the member states, you can travel more freely bringing back a wide range of goods from the continent, and the money you use abroad is now in the form of a new currency.

The EU and you

Let's see how the EU affects us in our daily lives. Sarah Miller is getting ready for school. Look closely at her routine set out in Figure **A**, and see how the EU affects her life.

As you can see, the EU affects us all every day. A few more of the benefits are described below.

Travelling within the EU

Since the opening of the **single market** in 1993, you can travel very easily to any country within the EU, and all member countries use a European passport. When you return from holiday you can bring goods back without having to pay any taxes. If you fall ill whilst visiting another EU country you are entitled to medical care there.

Studying in the EU

There are many exchange and study programmes available for students, which means that you can study abroad or become involved in a work experience programme in another country.

Figure A

7.30 am

Get up for school. When you have a shower, you can be sure that the water is clean and healthy because European Commission (EC) water quality standards make sure that the water has been tested and is safe for human consumption.

7.45 am

Make toast. You can be sure that the toaster is safe because EC regulations make sure that all electrical appliances meet strict safety standards. You can also be sure that your food is of a high quality because the EC demands that all foods are properly labelled with a list of all ingredients and additives.

8.10 am

Get on the school bus. You can be sure that you will get to school safely because the EC has laid down regulations that all exhaust fumes meet strict standards.

9.00 am

French lesson. If we are to be truly European it is essential that we have knowledge of a language other than English. In the future this could open up all sorts of educational and employment opportunities.

4.00 pm

School bus takes you home past a local farm. EU money is given to farmers to help them produce food cheaply and to help rural populations to survive.

▲ A session of the European Parliament in Brussels.

Working in the EU

You are entitled to work in another EU country for up to six months if you have a residence permit. Your qualifications should be recognised by the country in which you choose to stay.

Environmental protection

The members of the EU work together to solve environmental problems. This means that wildlife is protected, the quality of the air that we breathe is tested, and our beaches are subject to strict controls to ensure that we are all protecting our environment and are protected ourselves.

4.15 pm

You notice that the main road at the end of your street is closed because of workmen. The sign displayed on the road tells you that EU money is being used to improve the road surface.

5.00 pm

Your parents tell you the good news! Your dad's firm has opened a branch in Spain and the family will emigrate soon. This is because the EU allows freedom of movement. You now look forward to a new life abroad in the sun.

Figure Ⓑ

DAILY CRIER
Europe is Booming!
The European Union is booming – and it's official. Figures released today point out that members of the EU are benefiting. Countries like Portugal and Ireland have received much help with their roads and housing, whilst most countries have better food and safety standards as a result of EU regulations. Many other countries are now keen to join – but some members are worried that enlarging the EU might lead to problems.

SUMMARY

Many European citizens benefit from European Union membership.

EU rules and laws affect us every day.

Travelling, working and studying in another European country are much easier now that we have the EU.

The EU works to protect our environment.

ACTIVITIES

1   Name three benefits of EU membership when travelling abroad.

2   Look at Figure Ⓐ. List the ways in which the EU affects Sarah Miller's life.

3   In what ways can European citizens benefit when studying in the EU?

4   What benefits are there for workers in the EU?

5   List the ways in which the EU protects our environment.

6   Look carefully at Figure Ⓑ. What evidence is there to suggest that 'Europe is Booming'?

7   'Many members are worried that enlarging the EU might lead to problems.'
    Can you think of any reason why making the EU larger could lead to problems?

5.12 Why do we need pressure groups?

What is a pressure group?

We can participate in a democracy in many different ways:

■ by voting in elections

■ by standing as a candidate in an election

■ by being elected to represent people as an MP, MSP, MEP or a councillor.

But what happens when you don't agree with a decision that has been made by a representative in the government or the local council, or if you want a large organisation to change its mind on an issue that affects you?

In a democracy, people can form pressure groups in these situations.

A **pressure group** is a group of people who come together because they feel strongly about an issue and would like to put pressure on organisations, such as the government, to make changes. Sometimes they want to see new laws being made, or they may simply want to see improved facilities for particular groups of people. Unlike a political party, pressure groups deal with just a single issue. Their main role is to influence decisions made by governments or large organisations. There are two main types of pressure group:

■ **Promotional groups**

These put forward a particular viewpoint. People join these groups because they agree with the aims of the group. Examples include Help the Aged, and Shelter.

■ **Sectional groups**

These groups exist to protect the interests of a particular section of society. People join these groups because they have shared interests. Trade unions are the best-known examples of sectional groups. Examples include UNISON, and the SSTA (Scottish Secondary Teachers Association).

Why do we need pressure groups?

Pressure groups are important in a democracy. They enable people to speak out for their beliefs. A group of people working together for a cause is much stronger than a protest by an individual. Pressure groups can be very powerful. At national level, they can sometimes be responsible for making the government change certain policies. Locally, a pressure group may put pressure on local bodies to change a decision, for example on the closure of a school.

What methods do pressure groups use?

Pressure groups want as many people as possible to know about their cause. So they use several different methods to draw attention to their cause. Figure Ⓐ shows some of these methods.

Figure Ⓐ

- A pressure group may hold a **demonstration**.

- The group hope their demonstration will be shown on the **news on television** or be **reported in newspapers**, as this could bring more public support.

- The group can organise **petitions** for people to sign and hand in to the local council or other interested organisations, in order to persuade officials to change a decision.

- **Television advertising** and **internet websites** are a popular way of attracting attention – and donations to the cause – because they reach a large number of people.

- The group can **post leaflets** through doors, put up **posters** and hold **public meetings** to attract attention to the cause.

- Members of the group can **contact an MP** to speak on behalf of their cause. The MP may be able to take action to help the pressure group outside or inside Parliament.

Some pressure groups organise special stunts to gain publicity. For example, Greenpeace may send a ship to try to stop a country dumping nuclear waste at sea, whilst some animal rights groups attract attention to their cause by attacking animal laboratories. However, such activities often involve people in breaking the law.

▼ The Greenpeace ship *Rainbow Warrior* prevents British military ships from loading with supplies for the Gulf, in 2003.

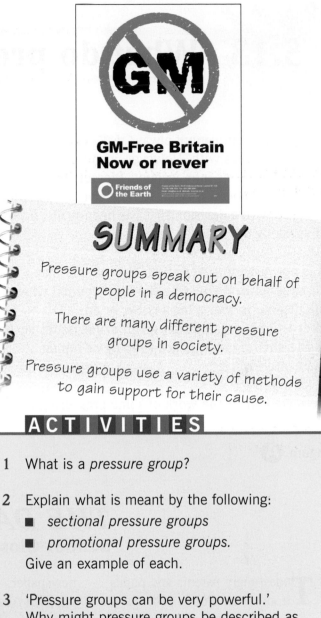

GM-Free Britain
Now or never

○ Friends of the Earth

SUMMARY

Pressure groups speak out on behalf of people in a democracy.

There are many different pressure groups in society.

Pressure groups use a variety of methods to gain support for their cause.

ACTIVITIES

1 What is a *pressure group*?

2 Explain what is meant by the following:
 ■ *sectional pressure groups*
 ■ *promotional pressure groups.*
 Give an example of each.

3 'Pressure groups can be very powerful.' Why might pressure groups be described as powerful?

4 Copy and complete the table below. The first example has been completed for you. Fill in three more methods that pressure groups use to draw attention to their cause. Explain the reasons for using each of these methods.

Method	Reasons for using this method
Demonstration	To gain the public's attention for their cause

5 Find out more about one particular pressure group. You could visit a website on the internet to carry out this task.

5.13 What do pressure groups do?

The government cannot always make decisions that everyone agrees with. However, it should take people's opinions into account. Pressure groups are vital in a democracy, because they give people who disagree with a decision that has been made, a way of speaking out.

It is not just the government that people may disagree with. It could be the local council when the dispute is over a local issue, or an international organisation when major issues such as the environment, peace-keeping or human rights are involved.

Here we look at the work of some pressure groups in action.

Figure Ⓐ

Local pressure groups

Figure Ⓐ highlights a local issue and the methods used by a small pressure group.

As you can see, the people of Aberneed were angered by the council decision so they decided to set up a pressure group to fight for their school. They made use of some of the typical pressure group methods to fight their campaign. People who live in democracies have the right to speak out.

Four months later, the newspaper article in Figure Ⓑ appeared in the local press.

As you can see, the power of a pressure group can make a big difference. But it's not just small local decisions where people can make a difference.

THE DAILY STING
School Closure 'On the Way'

Today angry parents and pupils from High Point Secondary, one of Aberneed's top secondary schools, gathered at council offices to protest at the proposed closure of the school next spring. The local council is planning to shut the school down and merge it with High Croft School at High Croft's current site. Protesters to the scheme have named themselves 'No More Closures'. The group numbered at least 500 people and shouted angrily at council chiefs as they entered the building to attend a meeting about the closures.

Mary White, leader of the group 'No More Closures', told this newspaper: 'The parents and pupils of Aberneed are outraged at this decision. Everyone knows that this is the best school in the area. Exam results are among the best in the country and the pupils do well in many other areas including football, athletics and debating. The council simply wants to save some money and we'll not allow this to happen!'

Speaking on behalf of the council, Charles French, Convenor of the Education Committee, defended the council's decision when he argued, 'The council has no option in this matter. We are aware of the school's excellent reputation but the school roll is falling and the site at High Croft is much larger and can easily accommodate both schools. Added to that, the council plans to provide brand-new computer and sports facilities at the new site which will benefit both the pupils and the local community.'

'No More Closures', the group fighting the campaign, vowed that they would continue to put pressure on the council. A protest has been organised in the town centre for next Saturday and a petition has already gathered over 5,000 signatures in support of their cause.

Figure **B**

National pressure groups

National issues are often contested by pressure groups. In recent years protestors have campaigned against nuclear weapons, the fur industry, and new road building. A recent example of a national issue is the ban on foxhunting. The Scottish Parliament has banned foxhunting in Scotland and the British Government is considering stopping or reducing foxhunting in England and Wales. Many people argue that foxhunting is cruel and unnecessary, whilst others say it is a necessary part of countryside living.

The pressure group called Countryside Alliance was set up to try to persuade the government to change its mind. It is involved in protest marches and campaigns on behalf of people in the countryside. In September 2002 almost 400,000 people marched through London to show the government how they felt. Around 20 roads in central London were closed to traffic and 1,600 police officers were on duty to keep order.

This protest showed the government that many people are behind the pressure group.

SUMMARY

Pressure groups act at local, national and international levels.

They can often gain a great deal of publicity by their actions.

The actions of pressure groups can often result in change being made.

ACTIVITIES

1 (a) Read Figure **A** again.
   (b) Why are the parents angry with the council?

2 Using the information in the newspaper article, copy and complete the table below, providing arguments for and *against* closing the school.

Arguments for	Arguments against

3 What methods has the pressure group used to promote its cause?

4 'This was a great victory for the people.'
   Why was the decision on High Point Secondary considered 'a great victory'?

5 Can you think of a reason to explain why the council made 'no comment' on the decision?

6 Why was the Countryside Alliance national pressure group set up?

7 Do you think the government should be worried by the success of Countryside Alliance? Give reasons for your answer.

8 You might like to investigate the work of a pressure group. Try to think of ways in which you could do this, then write a report based on your findings.

6.1 What is the media?

In Britain today we are surrounded by it. Most homes use it every day, and our ability to obtain information depends upon it. But what is 'media'?

What is meant by media?

Media is a general term for several different ways of communicating with large numbers of people. In recent years the media has become a massive industry in Britain. We see media all around us. Most adults read a daily newspaper, almost every home in Britain today has at least one television, we listen to the radio in our cars, and we log on to the internet in our schools, libraries and homes.

More recently, the arrival of cable and digital television has greatly increased the amount of information available from our televisions, and faster, more effective internet connections mean that most of us can access information from across the world at any time in our homes.

INTERNET

RADIO

But which of these is the most popular form of media today? Newspapers are found in almost every home. But why are they important to us? Let's find out more about newspapers.

NEWSPAPERS

TELEVISION

MAGAZINES

Newspapers

Newspapers are quite cheap and many homes in Britain buy at least one every day to keep up to date with news, events or even celebrity gossip! What newspapers are bought in *your* home?

There are two main types of newspaper: tabloids and broadsheets.

- **Tabloids** generally report news and events in less detail than broadsheets. These newspapers tend to be smaller in size and their front pages usually show eye-catching headlines and pictures.

- **Broadsheets** usually include more in-depth articles. They are larger, and have more factual headlines.

Table **A** lists examples of each type of newspaper.

Table A

Broadsheets	Tabloids
The Herald	Daily Record
The Scotsman	The Sun
The Guardian	Daily Mirror
Daily Telegraph	Daily Star
The Sunday Times	News of the World
Scotland on Sunday	Sunday Mail
The Sunday Herald	Sunday Mirror

Popularity

The *News of the World* is the most popular Sunday newspaper in Britain today. It is a tabloid and its headlines generally focus on topical issues and celebrities' lives. Its sister paper, *The Sun*, is the most popular daily newspaper and has a similar content. Tables **B** and **C** show the circulation (readership) figures for the most popular newspapers in Britain today.

Table B

National Sunday newspaper circulation,
September 2002

News of the World	4,067,205
Sunday Mirror	1,804,334
People	1,301,700
Daily Star Sunday	719,308
Sunday Mail	656,921
Mail on Sunday	2,306,911
Sunday Express	910,177
Sunday Times	1,387,182
Sunday Telegraph	744,023

Table C

National daily newspaper circulation,
September 2002

The Sun	3,733,052
Daily Mirror	2,130,859
Daily Star	855,880
Daily Record	540,886
The Daily Mail	2,387,149
Daily Express	942,842
Daily Telegraph	934,527
The Times	640,424
The Guardian	389,894

Look carefully at these tables. Which type of newspaper is most popular in Britain today? Can you think why this might be the case?

As you can see, some newspapers are more popular than others. Many people buy particular newspapers because their size is more convenient; some people may have little interest in soap stars and film gossip, whilst others may wish to read more local or Scottish stories and buy a newspaper which reflects this. For this reason, the *Daily Record* and *Sunday Mail* are very popular newspapers in Scotland because their content tends to have a Scottish theme. Similarly, *Scotland on Sunday* has a very small circulation in England. People obviously choose their newspaper according to their own interests and views.

SUMMARY

Media is a way of communicating with large numbers of people.

Television, newspapers, the internet and radio are the most common forms of media.

Newspapers are very powerful forms of media.

ACTIVITIES

1   What is meant by *media*?

2   Why are newspapers the most common forms of media?

3   Copy and complete the following table, using the information below, to describe the two main types of newspaper.

Tabloid	Broadsheet

- ■ *factual*
- ■ *eye-catching*
- ■ *fewer pictures*
- ■ *less serious*

4   Name the three most popular national daily newspapers in the UK.

5   Why is the *Daily Record* a very popular newspaper in Scotland?

6   'The *News of the World* is a terrible paper. It has very little factual news and, as a result, very few people buy it.'
   What evidence is there to suggest that this is a biased statement?

7   *Class exercise*
   As a class, collect examples of tabloid and broadsheet newspapers. When you have done this, gather information relating to size, number of news stories, amount of advertising space, pictures and headlines. You could compile your results on charts and present them as spreadsheets on a computer.

85

6.2 How powerful is the media?

Power of the media

How powerful is the media? You might think that a television is simply a box that sits in the corner of the room – but let's see if it does actually have any influence on our lives.

Table

Percentage of 16–24 year olds using different forms of media (1999)

Watch TV	99%
Listen to radio	59%
Log on to the internet	88%

Table Ⓐ shows that the percentage of 16–24 year olds using media is very high. Almost everyone watches TV, and many young people access the internet for information.

Giving people information can be a source of power. The decision about what to tell and what to keep from people means that you can sometimes actually affect the way people think.

Media bias

A newspaper or television news programme can choose the stories it wants to cover. More importantly, it can decide how it wants to tell the story. In other words, it might put a slant on a story, meaning that it reports the story in a biased way. (Look back at pages 10–11 for more on bias.) Having the ability to reach millions of people who will believe what you say, is a very strong form of power.

Figures Ⓑ and Ⓒ show how newspapers have the power to influence how people think.

Figure Ⓑ

DAILY SHOUT

Give Our Firefighters a Pay Rise

Britain's firefighters today began a strike for the first time in 25 years. Our brave firefighters simply want a decent living wage to support their families whilst they carry out a very difficult and dangerous job protecting the lives of millions of British citizens.

Figure Ⓒ

DAILY WHINE

Firefighters Picket While Homes Burn

The strike, which began today by firefighters across Britain, is a national disgrace! Two people died whilst the army tried to put out fires in the north of Scotland. Firefighters, meanwhile, sit on picket lines and allow this tragedy to continue.

As you can see, the *Daily Shout* is very much in favour of the firefighters' strike, whilst the *Daily Whine* is against the strike. Obviously readers of these stories can make up their own minds but the use of bias and selective use of facts in both stories will affect many readers' views.

Media ownership

Many people believe that media ownership is very important in considering the power of newspapers. Most newspapers in Britain are owned by a small number of companies. Table **D** shows ownership of newspapers in Britain.

Table D

Owner	Newspaper
Mirror Group	Daily Mirror
	The Independent
	Daily Record
	Sunday Mail
News International	The Sun
	The Times
	Sunday Times
SMG	The Herald
	Evening Times
	Scottish Television

▲ Rupert Murdoch, owner of News International.

As you can see, a small number of companies own several different newspapers. Similarly, television and internet companies are often owned by large multinational corporations which are keen to influence the way people think.

Newspapers and television stations are usually run as businesses, so it is very important that they make a profit. For newspapers, this means high circulation figures; for news programmes it means large viewing figures. To make more money, most newspapers sell space for advertising, and television stations do the same. Advertising companies may also influence how newspapers and radio stations are run.

Ownership of the media gives a small number of people a great deal of power. In a democracy it is very important that we do not allow them to become too powerful. The government may stop a company from buying up more newspapers as this could lead to that company becoming too powerful.

SUMMARY

The media has a very powerful influence on our lives.

The media can influence people's views.

Most forms of media are owned by a small number of companies which need to make a profit..

ACTIVITIES

1   Look carefully at Table **A**.
    (a) Which is the most popular form of media used by 16–24 year olds?
    (b) Which is the least popular form of media used by 16–24 year olds?

2   Look carefully at Figures **B** and **C**.
    (a) Which of these newspapers is biased *for* the firefighters? Give evidence from the source in your answer.
    (b) Which of these newspapers is biased *against* the firefighters? Give evidence from the source in your answer.

3   (a) Name three important media groups in Britain today.
    (b) For each group, state the names of the forms of media that they own.

4   How do television stations make money?

5   What role does the government play in keeping control on the media?

Can the media influence election results?

The media and election campaigns

When people vote in an election, very often the decision they make is influenced by what they have seen or heard in the media. There are strict rules on what can be broadcast on television and radio, so these forms of media are less likely to be biased during elections than newspapers.

Political parties are given set amounts of time on TV during an election campaign, to make sure that no single party has more time than others. We usually see political campaigns on TV in the form of party political broadcasts. These give parties the chance to have their say on TV during an election campaign.

Newspapers and elections

During elections, newspapers often back one party to win. Their stories often make one party look good and the others look bad.

Until the 1997 General Election, most newspapers would side with the Conservative Party. But in the run-up to the 1997 election, many papers began to favour the Labour Party led by Tony Blair.

Newspaper support can be very good for a party during election time. Table **A** shows the support for the two main parties, the Labour Party and the Conservative Party, in the 1997 and 2001 election campaigns.

Table

Party preference of newspapers, 1997 and 2001

	1997	2001
The Sun	Labour	Labour
Daily Express	Conservative	Labour
Daily Mail	Conservative	Conservative
The Daily Mirror	Labour	Labour
The Independent	Labour	Labour
Daily Telegraph	Conservative	Conservative
The Guardian	Labour	Labour

With a large number of newspapers supporting the Labour Party, the electorate were reading a lot of information that said good things about Labour. Photographs showed Tony Blair and his family looking happy and confident, and any stories praised the Labour Party.

Look carefully at Figures **B** and **C**.

Figure

Yesterday, Tony Blair, leader of the Labour Party, and his wife Cherie were looking radiant as they met with crowds of happy supporters on a walkabout in Aberneed. People waved flags supporting the Labour Party and Tony and his wife shook hands with the crowd as they made their way to the town centre to address a rally attended by thousands of well-wishers.

Figure

Iain Duncan Smith, leader of the Conservative Party, addressed crowds of cheering supporters at a meeting of the Aberneed Conservative Party. He was met with a huge round of applause, and banners of support for the party leader were displayed around the hall.

As you can see, each of these reports is biased in favour of a political party. This is typical of the type of reporting we see in newspapers just before a General Election. Newspaper support can be important for a political party.

The biggest change for the Labour Party in 1997 was when *The Sun*, the largest selling newspaper, changed its support from the Conservatives to the Labour Party. This meant that *The Sun*'s readers read good things about the Labour Party and perhaps not such good things about the Conservative Party.

When the Conservatives won the 1992 election, *The Sun* carried the headline 'It was the Sun wot won it'. Five years later, after *The Sun* had switched its support to the Labour Party, it carried the headline 'It's my son wot won it', with a picture of Tony Blair's dad. Can you think what this meant?

The media helps people to make decisions, so obviously the way in which news is reported is very important, especially during election time. Some people say that Labour won the election because of *The Sun*'s support for the party! Others, though, would say that *The Sun* switched to support Labour because it was clear that Labour was going to win.

Bad press

Sometimes news that is bad for a political party can be good for a newspaper. In the 2001 election campaign, John Prescott, a Labour politician, punched a protester whilst he was campaigning for the Labour Party in Rhyl, Wales. The very next day, there was an increase in sales of newspapers by 130,000 as people bought papers to read all about it! Obviously, political parties that prefer to look good for the voters do not like this sort of publicity.

▲ John Prescott MP under attack.

SUMMARY

Media can influence the decisions people make on election day.

Many newspapers present biased views in their reports.

Sometimes bad reports during an election campaign can affect results.

ACTIVITIES

1   Which forms of media are less likely to be biased during an election campaigns? Explain your answer.

2   Name the newspaper that switched from Conservative to Labour in the 2001 election campaign. Can you suggest why this happened?

3   Name four newspapers that supported Labour in both the 1997 and 2001 campaigns.

4   Why is newspaper support very important for a political party during an election campaign?

5   Look carefully at Figures **B** and **C**.
    (a) Which newspaper supports Labour? Pick out words or phrases from the report to explain your answer.
    (b) Which newspaper supports the Conservatives? Pick out words or phrases from the report to explain your answer.

6.4 What is freedom of the press?

> Everyone has the right to the freedom of opinion and expression; this right includes freedom to hold opinions without interference and to seek, receive and impart information and ideas through any media, regardless of frontiers.
>
> *Universal Declaration of Human Rights*

We live in a democracy and we have freedom of speech. We also have freedom of the press. In other words, the media has the right to provide information which people want to know.

In a democracy it is very important that we have these freedoms. Freedom of the press allows us to read information that is not controlled by the government. We can then make up our own mind about issues.

However, this freedom can often be abused by the media to try and make us think in a particular way. Many people believe everything they read in newspapers and if the information is not accurate then the public can believe information that is not the truth.

Can we control the media?

Some people find themselves being the targets of bad publicity by the press. Famous people (celebrities) may find themselves being photographed as they do their shopping or even when they are sunbathing on holiday. Sometimes newspapers print things they know are untrue, in a bid to sell more newspapers.

The **Press Complaints Commission** was set up to stop this, and to help protect people. It has a **Press Code,** and people writing stories for the media are expected to follow its guidelines (Figure **A**).

Figure A The Press Code

- Newspapers must not publish inaccurate information or pictures.

- Newspapers should protect people's privacy and family life.

- Newspapers must avoid prejudice.

- Newspapers must not harass people for information.

- Newspapers must not intrude on children during their schooling.

However, newspapers have one main aim and that is to sell as many papers as possible. If a journalist or photographer thinks that their work will sell newspapers, then often these guidelines are ignored. Can you think of anyone whose privacy has been invaded by the press in recent years?

Is it ever right to control the media?

One example of government control of the media was during the Falklands War in 1981. During this war between Britain and Argentina there was a complete news blackout. This meant that the only information given to the public was strictly controlled by the government. Every night, a government spokesperson appeared on television and in a slow and serious manner described events as the government thought we should know them.

In a democracy it is only at such times of national security that the government controls the power of the press. However, in some other countries, such as dictatorships, the media is owned and controlled by the government. This means that people only learn about what the government wants them to know, and often that information is incorrect.

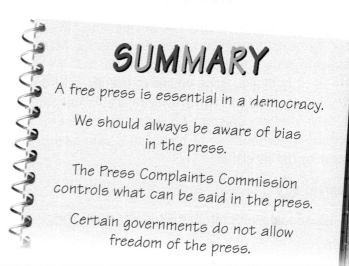

SUMMARY

A free press is essential in a democracy.

We should always be aware of bias in the press.

The Press Complaints Commission controls what can be said in the press.

Certain governments do not allow freedom of the press.

ACTIVITIES

1 Why is freedom of the press essential in a democracy?

2 Why was the Press Complaints Commission set up?

3 (a) List the rules that newspapers should follow under the Press Code.
(b) Why do some newspapers often ignore the Press Code?

4 'Governments need to control the media during difficult times.'
Why might governments decide to control the media?

5 *Opinion polls*
Carry out a survey of opinions on the media among your class.
Here are some examples of questions that you might ask:

How often do you read a newspaper?	Every day	Weekly	Not at all
Which newspaper do you read?			
Are you aware of bias in newspapers?	Yes	No	Don't know
Should governments be allowed to control media?	Yes	No	Don't know

Once you have collated the results you can present your findings on bar graphs or store them on spreadsheets on a computer. They can then be used as a wall display on which you can describe and explain your findings.

6.5 How important is the internet?

Using the internet

In recent years, the number of people who have access to the internet has risen dramatically. Many homes in Britain now have access to the net. We use it to book holidays, write emails to friends, sort out our finances – and to investigate topical issues for Modern Studies. Diagram Ⓐ shows the recent increase in the number of households who have access to the internet.

Diagram Ⓐ

UK households with internet access, 1999–2002

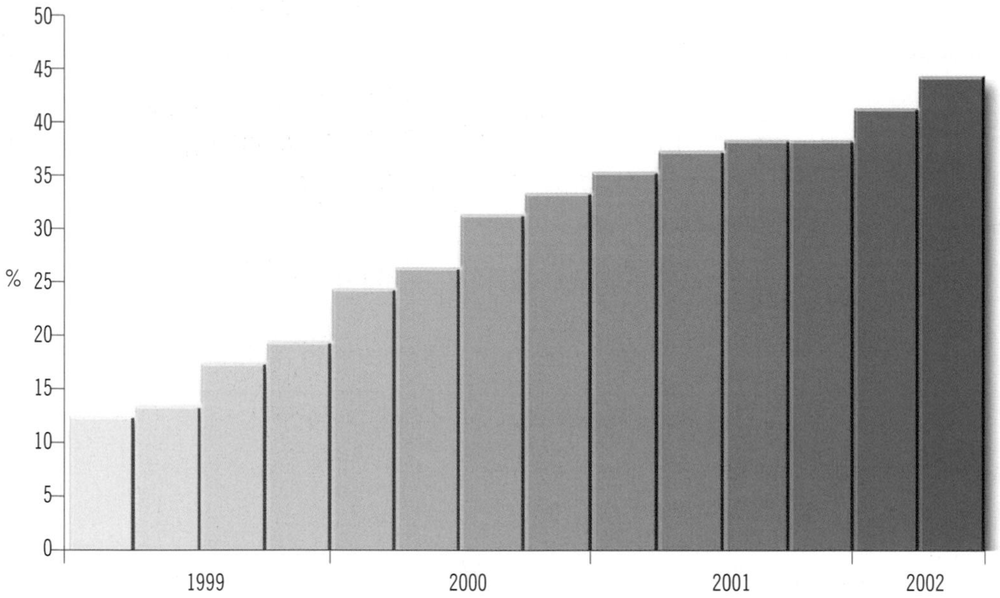

As you can see, the number of people who have access to the internet has increased rapidly in recent years. In 2002, 45% of homes in Britain had access to the internet compared with 38% in 2001. If people are to participate in a democracy then they must be properly informed. The internet can provide a great deal of information, ideas and arguments. In countries where people are not free, the internet can help people find out about what is happening in the world. But in some countries where the government wants to control the lives of its people, internet access is strictly limited.

How useful *is* the internet?

For students of Modern Studies, the internet has opened up a huge amount of information from across the world. The internet is therefore a very important form of media.

Every political party has its own website, and newspapers allow you to download information from their past editions. As a student of Modern Studies you might be interested in the following sites:

www.labour.org.uk
www.conservatives.com
www.greenparty.org.uk
www.libdems.org.uk
www.snp.org.uk
www.scottishsocialistparty.org
www.parliament.gov.uk
www.scottishparliament.gov.uk

◀ Many people go to an internet café to access the World Wide Web.

Your teacher may ask you to carry out research on a topical issue for a Modern Studies investigation. By making use of the internet you will have a wide choice of information from websites across the world. For example:

- If you wish to find out about the American System of government, you might visit a website such as:

  www.whitehouse.com

- Perhaps you want to gather useful statistics on living standards in Britain. To do this, a useful website could be:

  www.statistics.gov.uk

- Or maybe you just want to read the latest edition of a national daily newspaper. A useful site would be:

  www.guardianunlimited.co.uk

There are many advantages to students carrying out investigations using the internet but there are also disadvantages. Some of these are listed in Table **B**.

Table B

Using the internet for investigating

Advantages	Disadvantages
Quick access to information	Need access to a computer
Easy to download information	Some sources of information are unreliable
You can email people direct	Can be expensive to use

Control of the internet

There is very little to prevent people putting unsuitable or even illegal material on the web. Your parents may have installed a monitoring service on your home computer to make sure that you cannot access unsuitable material, and your school will certainly have controls over what you download.

However, as Modern Studies students you will be aware of the need to look carefully at any information that is presented to you. We need to be especially careful when looking on the internet, as often we do not know the source of information – it may be biased, exaggerated or simply downright lies! We should always be careful to stick to well-known sites.

The internet is an increasingly important form of media, but it needs to be used with care.

▼ Home page of the SNP website.

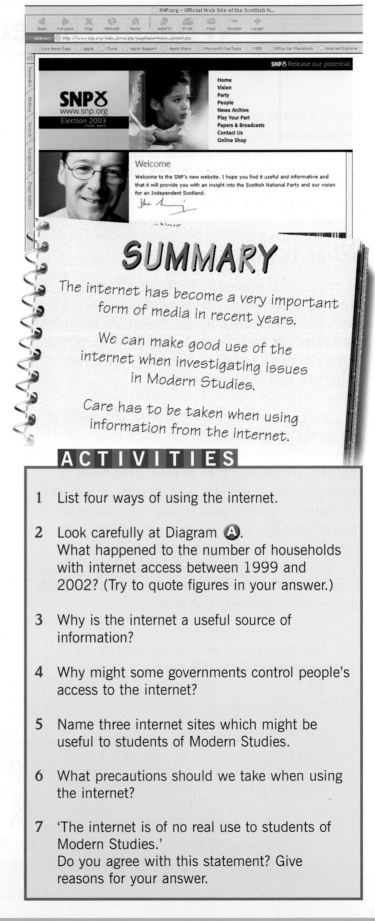

SUMMARY

The internet has become a very important form of media in recent years.

We can make good use of the internet when investigating issues in Modern Studies.

Care has to be taken when using information from the internet.

ACTIVITIES

1 List four ways of using the internet.

2 Look carefully at Diagram **A**. What happened to the number of households with internet access between 1999 and 2002? (Try to quote figures in your answer.)

3 Why is the internet a useful source of information?

4 Why might some governments control people's access to the internet?

5 Name three internet sites which might be useful to students of Modern Studies.

6 What precautions should we take when using the internet?

7 'The internet is of no real use to students of Modern Studies.' Do you agree with this statement? Give reasons for your answer.

7.1 What is the economy?

People's needs are not only met by the government; the **economy** also has a vital role to play in meeting people's needs. This unit looks at the ways the economy meets – and sometimes fails to meet – people's needs at home in Scotland, and in the rest of the world.

What is an economy?

An economy is made up of consumers and producers. Each one of us is a consumer because we buy goods that meet our basic needs. As **consumers** we satisfy our basic needs by buying food, housing and clothing. Consumers, therefore, are a very important part of an economy.

Producers are individuals or groups who make or supply the goods and services which consumers buy. Shop and factory workers, farmers, miners and teachers are all examples of producers. Each of these producers provides useful goods or services. For example, a shop worker may sell clothes, a farmer produces food, while teachers sell their knowledge and skills in return for a salary.

Economics, therefore, is concerned with the study of consumers (buyers) and producers.

▼ A Virgin train, part of the huge company set up by the entrepreneur Richard Branson.

How does the economy meet people's needs?

Most economies have a private sector and a public sector. In Britain, most of the goods and services that are bought are produced in the private sector.

The private sector

The private sector consists of individuals and companies that produce goods in order to make a profit. They help to meet people's needs in a number of ways.

■ **Providing jobs**

Private companies create thousands of jobs in Britain. People who set up their own companies are called **entrepreneurs**. People like Richard Branson, who set up Virgin Airline, have created thousands of jobs in the process.

■ **Producing goods**

The private sector produces many different types of goods which help to meet people's needs. A whole range of goods from food and housing to televisions, CDs and computers are produced by the private sector.

■ **Producing cheaper goods**

New methods of production by private sector companies has meant that goods can be produced more cheaply, so they can be sold more cheaply too. When the price of goods is low, people are more willing to buy the goods. The private sector therefore helps to meet people's needs by producing goods that people want and which they can afford to buy.

The public sector

The public sector is the goods and services that are produced by the government. The government usually produces goods and services to meet specific needs. For example, the National Health Service (NHS) is provided by the government and is designed to meet people's health needs through the provision of doctors, nurses and hospitals.

The government does not produce these goods to make a profit. Services produced by the public sector are mostly funded by taxation. There are many different types of taxes.

For example, **income tax** is paid by most individuals who have a job. The income tax rate currently stands at 22%. This means that for every £1 a worker makes they pay 22p to the government. This helps to pay for services provided by the government such as the police, healthcare and education.

SUMMARY

An economy is made up of producers and consumers.

Most economies consist of a public and a private sector.

The public and private sectors meet people's needs in a variety of ways.

ACTIVITIES

1 What is an *economy*?

2 What role do *consumers* and *producers* play in an economy?

3 Describe the main ways that the private sector meets people's needs.

4 In what ways does the public sector meet people's needs?

5 Working in pairs, write down as many different types of goods or services provided by the public sector that you can think of.

6 How does the public sector raise money to pay for the services it provides?

7 'In Britain, the public sector is not important.' Provide one piece of evidence which shows that the above statement is not true.

What makes people rich or poor in Britain?

Compared with many countries, Britain is very wealthy. Many people have jobs, live in good-quality housing and can afford to have luxury goods such as cars and mobile phones. In some less developed countries, even basic needs such as housing and healthcare are regarded as luxuries.

However, this does not mean that all people in Britain have the same level of income or wealth. For many people in Britain today poverty is a major problem, whilst others can afford a luxurious lifestyle.

For many people, highly paid professional jobs or self-employment have enabled them to have a good standard of living. They have comfortable homes and expensive cars, and take holidays abroad. For others, poorly paid jobs or living on benefits from the government means they have a poor standard of living. Such people tend to live in poor-quality housing in run-down areas, they cannot afford to buy a car, and can only dream of luxuries such as going on holiday or owning a mobile phone.

But what evidence do we have of this inequality?

Rich and poor in Britain

The distribution of wealth in Britain today is very uneven – see Diagram **A**.

Diagram A

The balance of wealth in Britain

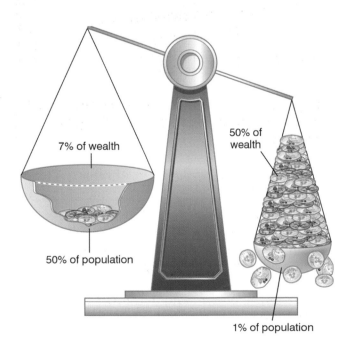

7% of wealth

50% of wealth

50% of population

1% of population

Poverty

Poverty has become a major problem for the British Government in recent years. One study states that the number of children living in poverty in Scotland has increased to almost one in three children. It also suggests that about a quarter of the Scottish population is living in poverty.

What causes poverty?

Diagram **B** shows some of the main causes of poverty.

Diagram B

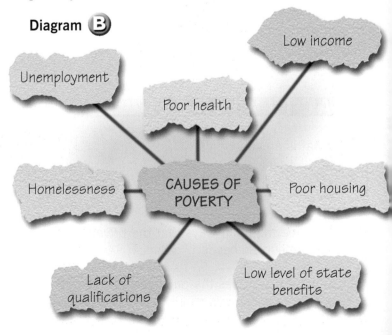

Unemployment

Low income

Poor health

Homelessness

CAUSES OF POVERTY

Poor housing

Lack of qualifications

Low level of state benefits

What problems does it cause?

Poverty causes many problems in our society. Often it is linked with poor examination results at school, health problems and crime. Poverty is therefore a major worry for the government.

Standard of living

An example of the gap between rich and poor can be seen when we compare life in two parts of Glasgow: Bearsden and Drumchapel. These are two areas in the north of Glasgow. Bearsden is regarded as an area where people enjoy a high standard of living, whilst only one mile away in Drumchapel there is much poverty. Some statistics state that people of a similar age are likely to live as much as 10 years longer if they live in Bearsden than those living in Drumchapel! This is due to the differences in their standard of living.

Poor housing

Poor housing causes many problems in Scotland. In recent years the price of housing has increased very quickly, which has allowed some people to become wealthy. However, for many other people, houses have become too expensive to buy. Areas such as the West End of Glasgow, and some areas of Edinburgh, have seen a massive increase in prices, which means that many people cannot afford to buy in these areas, whilst other areas have become very run-down.

Debt

For many people in Scotland today, **debt** is a huge problem. Recently, private companies have made loans seem very attractive to people, particularly those on a low income who cannot afford to buy luxuries when they need them. It is estimated that in 2002 the average Briton owed at least £2,300.

How does the government tackle poverty?

As a result of all of these problems, the government is constantly trying to combat poverty. To do this the **national minimum wage** was introduced. This guaranteed everyone a minimum level of income from employment. The welfare state also provides benefits for some people. However, often the government is criticised because, it is claimed, the minimum wage is not high enough, and the level of benefits is too low.

The problem of poverty in Scotland is huge and governments find it very difficult to provide a solution.

SUMMARY

There is a huge gap between rich and poor in Britain today.

Poverty is caused by a variety of factors.

Standards of living vary across Scotland.

The government takes steps to tackle poverty.

ACTIVITIES

1 Suggest how you could measure poverty – that is, whether people are well-off or living in poverty.

2 'Poverty is a huge problem for children living in Scotland.' *Child Poverty Action Group*

   What evidence is there to suggest that this statement is true?

3 Name five causes of poverty.

4 What problems can poverty cause in our society today?

5 What steps have governments taken to tackle poverty? Do you think these have worked? Give reasons for your answer.

What are more and less economically developed countries?

In Britain we take our economy for granted. A huge range of goods and services are produced and bought in Britain to meet people's needs. Britain's economy is also responsible for creating a great deal of wealth. Britain can be described as a **more economically developed country** (MEDC).

However, economies like Britain's do not exist in every part of the world. In many poor countries, people's basic needs are not met. In these countries people often suffer from starvation, poverty and illness, and have little access to education. These countries are described as **less economically developed countries** (LEDCs).

A North/South split?

MEDCs are mostly located in the northern half of the world ('the North'). Countries in Europe and

Diagram A

Where in the world are the LEDCs and the MEDCs?

North America tend to be MEDCs. Examples of these richer countries include Britain, France, Germany, Canada and the USA.

LEDCs are mostly located in the southern half of the world ('the South'). The continents of Africa and South America include many LEDCs. Asia also has a high concentration of LEDCs (Diagram A).

However, not every country in the North is rich, and not every country in the South is poor. For example, Australia and New Zealand are both wealthy countries, yet they are in the South – so there are some exceptions.

Comparing MEDCs and LEDCs

Several things can help us to compare rich and poor countries. For example, it is possible to compare life expectancy (the average age that people can expect to live to in a country) between a rich and a poor country. As you might expect, people in LEDCs have lower life expectancies than those in MEDCs.

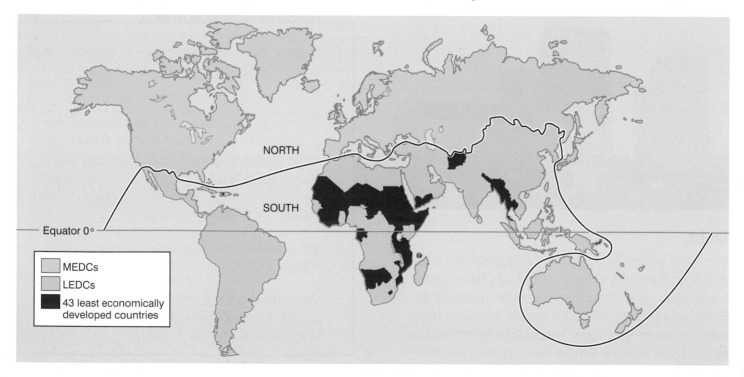

NORTH

SOUTH

Equator 0°

MEDCs
LEDCs
43 least economically developed countries

▲ A hurricane can have a disastrous effect on the economy of an LEDC.

What causes the problems faced by LEDCs?

Poverty, illness, starvation and a lack of education are all indicators of some of the problems facing LEDCs. These problems are caused by a number of connected issues.

Debt and international trading

In the 1970s, LEDCs had to borrow money from MEDCs to help meet their basic needs and to develop their own economies further. At the same time the price of crops that LEDCs produced decreased dramatically. LEDCs were forced to borrow more money from MEDCs. Today, many LEDCs are crippled by the debts they owe to rich countries in the world.

Political problems

Many LEDCs have an unstable government. **Civil wars** have made the problems faced by these countries worse. Corrupt governments in some LEDCs have spent the money borrowed from MEDCs on weapons and military equipment, rather than on items that are needed to meet people's basic needs, such as food, or schools.

Study Table **B**. It compares some important indicators in the African country of Uganda, and in the UK.

Table **B**

	Uganda	UK
People		
Population	23.3	59.4
Life expectancy (years)	44.0	77.7
Infant mortality (deaths per 1,000)	81	6
Education		
Adult literacy (% adult population who can read)	67.1	99
Economic and social		
Average income (US$ per head)	300	21,410
Internet users (thousands in 2000)	25	19,470
Daily calorie intake per head	2,238	3,237

Natural disasters

Many of the problems faced by LEDCs have been made worse by natural disasters. Severe droughts have resulted in less food being grown, and less safe drinking water being available.

SUMMARY

MEDCs are richer countries which are mostly located in the North.

LEDCs are poor countries which are mostly located in the South.

Problems such as debt, natural disasters, poverty, illness and wars affect LEDCs.

ACTIVITIES

1 Describe the difference between a more developed country and a less developed country.

2 'LEDCs are all located in the South.' Do you agree with this statement? Provide evidence to support your answer.

3 Use the information in Table **B** to write a report that describes the main differences between Uganda and the UK.

4 'Uganda has roughly the same infant mortality and life expectancy rates as the UK.' Why is this statement an exaggeration?

5 Write a couple of paragraphs which explain the main problems faced by LEDCs.

6 *Internet/library research* Select an African country of your choice and compare it with the UK in the following key areas:
- *Population*
- *Average income*
- *Life expectancy*
- *Infant mortality*
- *Adult literacy.*

Write a report describing the main differences between your chosen country and the UK.

7.4 What is the global economy?

Globalisation describes the increasing number of ways in which countries rely on each other throughout the world. One way that countries rely on each other is through trading.

In today's world, goods can be produced and bought in any part of the world. Each country's own economy is linked with the economies of many other countries. This process is not a new one. Nations have traded with each other for hundreds of years. However, a number of recent developments have increased the degree to which countries rely on each other.

Why has globalisation taken place?

Improvements in communications and transport

The world is now a much smaller place as a result of improvements in communications and transport. Air travel means that people and goods can be transported across the world quickly and cheaply. Technological advances have also made countries more interdependent. For example, people can now purchase goods via the internet from virtually any part of the world.

Multinational companies

A **multinational company** or **corporation** is one that conducts its business in more than one country. There are thousands of these companies throughout the world today: Pepsi, Nike, Adidas, Microsoft and IBM are all multinationals. Between them, multinational companies account for a large proportion of the

▲ The McDonalds restaurant in Beijing, China.

world's total trade. In fact, some multinational companies are wealthier than some poor countries.

There are many advantages for multinationals operating in more than one country. For example, it gives them access to new consumers who will buy their products. Many multinationals also take advantage of lower wages in poor countries and set up factories there. This cuts their costs and increases their profits.

However, many people are concerned about the role of multinational companies in the global economy. There are several reasons for this.

- Multinationals are accused of exploiting people in poor countries because they employ workers on wages that are too low and in working conditions that are unacceptable.

- Multinationals are accused of having no long-term commitment to the countries in which they operate. If it is cheaper to close a factory and locate it in another country, a multinational will do so. This often results in sudden unemployment. Many jobs in Scotland depend on the decisions of multinational companies. In recent years several have closed their factories in Scotland in order to move production to countries where wages and costs are lower.

- Multinational companies have been criticised for their lack of concern about the environment. They are accused of polluting the environment with waste produced by their factories across the world.

Diagram Ⓐ sets out the arguments for and against the process of globalisation.

Diagram Ⓐ

Globalisation – the debate

For	Against
Jobs are created across the world.	Multinational companies benefit the most from globalisation.
Goods can be produced and consumed across the world.	Workers in poor countries are paid low wages and have poor working conditions.
Countries work closer together with each other.	The environment suffers from globalisation.

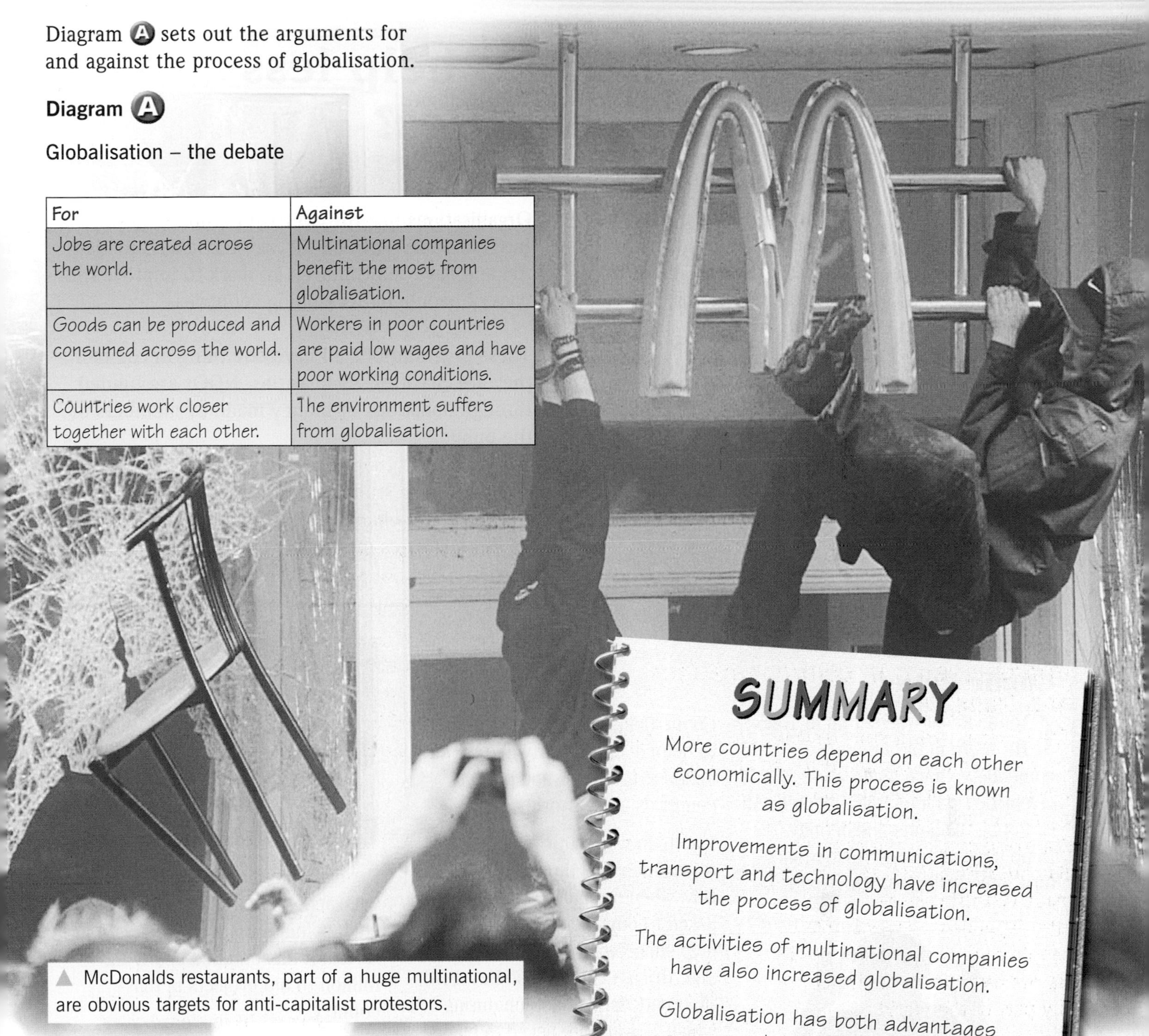

▲ McDonalds restaurants, part of a huge multinational, are obvious targets for anti-capitalist protestors.

SUMMARY

More countries depend on each other economically. This process is known as globalisation.

Improvements in communications, transport and technology have increased the process of globalisation.

The activities of multinational companies have also increased globalisation.

Globalisation has both advantages and disadvantages.

ACTIVITIES

1 Explain what the term *globalisation* means.

2 Describe the reasons why globalisation has taken place.

3 (a) What is a multinational company?
  (b) Make a list of as many multinational companies as you can.

4 Why do multinational companies locate in many different countries?

5 'Multinational companies and the global economy are bad for poor countries.'
Do you agree with this statement? Provide evidence to support your view.

7.5 How do charities help less developed countries?

Poorer countries in the world often have to rely on rich countries and various national and international organisations to meet their basic needs. This help is known as *aid*. Aid can come in many forms, for example money, food or machinery.

How do charities help developing countries?

There are a large number of **non-governmental organisations** (NGOs) which try to raise money in order to help people in developing countries meet their needs.

Organisations like the Scottish Catholic International Aid Fund (SCIAF), Oxfam, Christian Aid and Save the Children all work to improve the lives of people in developing countries.

These organisations all have one thing in common – they are charities. As charities, NGOs are funded through donations of money made by members of the public.

Study the case studies Ⓐ and Ⓑ. They describe the ways that two charities have helped people in poorer countries meet their needs.

CASE STUDY Ⓐ

Comic Relief

Comic Relief was set up in 1985 by a group of famous comedians. Since its creation, celebrities such as Billy Connolly, Ali G, Robbie Williams and Johnny Depp have all helped raise money for Comic Relief over the years.

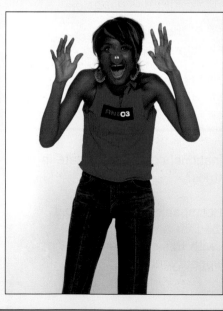

Comic Relief is seriously commited to helping end poverty and social injustice in the UK and poorest countries in the world.

The main way that Comic Relief raises money is through Red Nose Day, when ordinary people are asked to buy and wear a red nose to help children and families in Britain and Africa. On Red Nose Day, BBC TV broadcasts a telethon during which viewers are asked to pledge money to Comic Relief as the night unfolds. Since 1985 Comic Relief has raised almost 310 million.

The Comic Relief Children and Young's People's Fund works with some of the more vulnerable children around the world, by supporting education and attempting to tackle injustices like child slavery and the use of child soldiers..

For example, Comic Relief has been very active in tackling the use of child soldiers in Sierra Leone, in Africa. It has donated nearly £2 million to aid projects in that country.

One of these projects is called the Boys and Girls Society, which received over £72,000 from Comic Relief. Among other things, the project runs a six-month residential programme for former child soldiers between the ages of 12 and 18. During the programme these children are taught how to read and write – all thanks to the support of Comic Relief.

CASE STUDY **B**

SAVE THE CHILDREN

Save the Children is a charity which helps to provide aid to children throughout the world. The charity's £3 per month (or 10p a day) campaign aims to raise money to help children in over 70 countries. By donating £3 a month, the public can help Save the Children provide healthcare in the form of drugs and medicines, and expert training for health professionals. Save the Children is also active in providing education to children throughout the world, and in supplying emergency aid such as food and medical care when wars or natural disasters take place.

Photo: Dan White

10p a day can help save her life

The last few years have seen huge social and economic changes in Vientiane, capital of the Lao People's Democratic Republic. Drug abuse, promiscuity and sex before marriage are becoming more common. Poorly educated girls like Ket don't always have the skills to negotiate safe sex and are at real risk from HIV/AIDS infection.

To allow young peo[...] set up a drop-in ce[...] about drug abuse, [...] such as computing[...]

**10p a[...]
from [...]**

Save the Children

Just think what £3 a mo[...]

SUMMARY

Charities provide many different types of aid to LEDCs.

Examples of aid include providing teachers and helping former child soldiers.

Charities rely on fund-raising to pay for the aid they send to LEDCs.

ACTIVITIES

1 Look at case studies **A** and **B**.
   Describe how Comic Relief and Save the Children raise money.

2 Describe the ways that Comic Relief and Save the Children help people in developing countries.

3 *Classroom debate*
   'We should cancel the debt that LEDCs owe to the rich countries of the world.'

   ■ *Divide your class into two groups and debate this statement. One group should argue in favour of the statement. The other group should argue against the statement.*

   ■ *Appoint an opening and closing speaker for each group. The opening speakers should put forward their group's arguments at the beginning of the debate.*

   ■ *After the opening speeches anyone can put forward their point of view. Any points of view must be put through a chairperson.*

   ■ *At the end of the debate the closing speeches should summarise their groups' arguments.*

   ■ *The class should then vote on whether or not they are in favour of rich countries cancelling the debts of LEDCs.*

How do governments help less developed countries?

As well as charities, governments of the world's richer countries provide aid to developing countries. When the Labour Party won the General Election in 1997 it created the Department for International Development (DFID). The DFID is responsible for providing aid to poor countries in order to help them develop.

What is bilateral aid?

When Britain gives aid to an LEDC this is known as **bilateral aid**. Bilateral aid is aid given by one country to another. Types of aid could range from money, to sending teachers to educate children. Around half of all British aid is bilateral.

Britain also sends aid by giving money to non-governmental organisations (NGOs). The charity Save the Children is an NGO which provides aid to many LEDCs.

The remainder of British aid is given through international organisations like the United Nations and the European Union.

What is tied aid?

Bilateral aid has been criticised by some experts. This is because a lot of bilateral aid is 'tied'. **Tied aid** means that when a rich country gives aid, it demands that the poor country receiving the aid buys goods and services from the rich country in return. In other words, the rich country benefits from giving aid to the poor country. The British Government is now trying to ensure that its aid is not tied.

What is good aid?

Governments that give aid to developing countries are now trying to make sure that it is 'good aid'. Bad aid occurs when poor countries begin to rely on rich countries for their survival. For example, providing teachers and educational experts to poor countries is good, but poor countries must learn to train their own teachers. It is better that they do this themselves rather than constantly relying on rich countries.

▲ Girls being taught in a school in Kabul, Afghanistan.

▲ Famine victims in Africa.

The DFID in Ethiopia

Facfile Ⓐ

Location	Horn of Africa
Population	65 million
Average income (per year)	$100 Many people have to live on less than $1 per day
Life expectancy	43.4 years
Adult literacy (% of population who can read)	36.3%

The Horn of Africa

Background

As you can see from Factfile Ⓐ, Ethiopia is one of the poorest countries in the world. The country has suffered from a number of problems over the years.

■ In 1973 a severe drought struck Ethiopia. Just over 10 years later Ethiopia suffered large-scale famine, which prompted the musician Bob Geldof to set up the Live Aid fund-raising event.

■ In 1998 Ethiopia started a war with Eritrea, another country in the Horn of Africa. This war ended in 2000. Wars, poverty and natural disasters have all had a big impact on Ethiopia over the years.

How is the DFID helping Ethiopia?

The DFID expects to invest £30 million in Ethiopia between 2000 and 2003. This money is being spent in the following ways:

■ By giving £4 million over 5 years to improve roads in Ethiopia. This will help to make the transportation of food across the country easier.

■ By giving £5 million to help tackle the HIV/AIDS problem.

■ In 2000 the DFID gave 40,000 metric tonnes of food aid to Ethiopia.

■ The DFID is working closely with the Ethiopian Government to examine ways to reduce poverty.

You can find out more about the work of the DFID on its website:

www.dfid.gov.uk

SUMMARY

The Department for International Development (DFID) is responsible for giving British Government aid to LEDCs.

When one country gives aid to another country it is called bilateral aid.

The DFID supports developing countries in a number of ways.

ACTIVITIES

1 What is *bilateral aid*?

2 Why does *tied aid* benefit rich countries?

3 Describe the difference between *good aid* and *bad aid*.

4 Study Factfile Ⓐ.
What evidence is there that Ethiopia is a less economically developed country?

5 'Britain has done nothing to help Ethiopia.' Why is this statement inaccurate? Explain your answer.

7.7 How do international organisations help LEDCs?

A number of international organisations provide aid to developing countries. The United Nations (UN) and the European Union (EU) are two important international organisations involved in providing aid.

The United Nations (UN)

As well as campaigning for human rights and helping to end conflicts in the world, the UN works to help poorer countries. It gives aid to developing countries through its 'specialised agencies'. Diagram **A** shows some of the main UN agencies that help in developing countries.

Food and Agriculture Organisation (FAO)

The FAO works in developing countries to ensure that people have access to food. The FAO advises developing countries on the best ways to grow crops to ensure that food production is maintained. This advice could, for example, involve training local farmers to make the best use of their soil.

United Nations Educational, Scientific and Cultural Organisation (UNESCO)

In Burkina Faso, UNESCO is involved in providing basic education for people. Throughout Africa,

UNESCO is focusing on early childhood and family education, and trying to make sure that women and girls have greater access to education.

The United Nations Children's Emergency Fund (UNICEF)

UNICEF is involved in improving the health and education of children in developing countries. In Mali, UNICEF has been involved in immunising people against tetanus.

Diagram **A**

Some UN specialised agencies

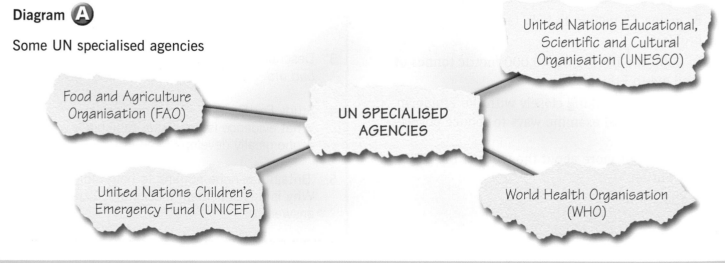

Food and Agriculture Organisation (FAO)

United Nations Children's Emergency Fund (UNICEF)

UN SPECIALISED AGENCIES

United Nations Educational, Scientific and Cultural Organisation (UNESCO)

World Health Organisation (WHO)

World Health Organisation (WHO)

The WHO is involved in the prevention and control of disease. It provides advice and assistance on issues such as clean water and sanitation. It also provides doctors, nurses and other medical experts who carry out vaccination programmes throughout the developing world.

The European Union (EU)

The EU has been involved in providing aid to developing countries since the 1950s. Today, the EU provides a large proportion of food aid to developing countries and is actually the largest giver of food aid in the world.

One way the EU provides help to developing countries is through humanitarian aid.

▲ Relief supplies are organised by the UN and the EU to destinations all over the world.

What is EU humanitarian aid?

Humanitarian aid is given to people who are the victims of natural disasters such as earthquakes or floods. Humanitarian aid is also given to people who have been the victims of human disasters such as wars or breakdowns in government.

There are three main types of humanitarian aid from the EU:

- **Emergency aid** is given to countries that have suffered from a disaster. Money is given for countries to buy items such as food, medicine and shelter.
- **Food aid** is given by the EU to countries that face famine. Emergency food aid is given to countries which face severe food shortages as a result of, for example, an earthquake or a war.
- **Refugee aid** – the EU gives aid to people who have been forced to move from their own country because of war or natural disasters, or because they are being persecuted.

SUMMARY

The UN and the EU are international organisations that give aid to poor countries.

The UN's specialised agencies all provide aid to poorer countries.

One way the EU helps LEDCs is by giving humanitarian aid.

ACTIVITIES

1   (a) Copy Diagram Ⓐ into your notebook.
    (b) Describe how each of the specialised agencies helps to meet the needs of people in poor countries.

2   For what reasons would the EU give humanitarian aid?

3   Describe the different types of EU humanitarian aid.

8.1 How do people's needs cause conflict?

An important feature of every society is that people are not all the same. They are different, because of race, religious beliefs, wealth, family background, what TV programmes they like, what music they enjoy – and so on!

People also have different wants and needs. For example, a homeless person's needs are different from those of someone living in their own home in warmth and comfort. A homeless person has to make sure that they have a roof over their head each night. For those with their own homes, this need has already been met.

What is conflict?

Sometimes when people have different wants and needs they fall out or argue with each other. When people disagree, there is **conflict**. Conflict can come in many different forms. It could be fighting with your brother or sister over which TV programme to watch – or it could be a war between two countries.

What is conflict resolution?

Most conflicts have one thing in common: sooner or later they have to end. Conflicts may last for hundreds of years, or be over in minutes.

▲ Israeli Prime Minister Ariel Sharon shakes hands with peace envoy General Anthony Zinni in Jerusalem before their meeting in November 2001.

When a conflict is over, it usually means that any disagreement, fighting or hostility between two or more groups has ended. The best way for a conflict to end is peacefully, fairly – and permanently.

Sometimes, two groups need the help of outsiders to act as go-betweens to resolve their disputes. Go-betweens talk to both sides and try to get them to solve their conflict. Most conflicts end when **concessions** have been made. This means each side has to give up some of its needs and wants so that the conflict can be resolved.

In this unit we look at different types of conflict, and at how they can, or have been, resolved. Here we look at a local conflict. The rest of the unit looks at conflict at different scales: on a national and an international basis.

Local conflict

Local conflicts take place in our communities all the time. Look at Figure , which describes a local conflict.

Figure Ⓐ

THE MILVERTON NEWS

Management and Workers in Conflict at Parsons

Parsons, the large car factory in Milverton, was in chaos yesterday after the management and workers failed to settle their differences. At the centre of the conflict between the management and the workers is the issue of pay and working conditions.

The workers are calling for a 15% pay increase and improved health and safety in the factory. The management will only agree to this if workers complete an extra 5 hours per week and accept cuts in the number of workers in the factory from 5,000 to 4,500 people.

Workers' leaders are now threatening to go on strike to get their demands met, while the management say they will sack any worker who strikes.

The disagreement at Parsons is typical of any conflict. Both sides have different needs, wants and opinions. To resolve this conflict both sides may have to give concessions to each other.

SUMMARY

People have different needs and wants. This often results in conflict.

Conflict occurs when two or more people or groups clash and cannot agree with each other.

Concessions are often made to resolve conflicts.

ACTIVITIES

1 Describe some of the ways in which people in society are different.

2 Describe some of the different needs that people have.

3 Explain what each of the following means:
   ■ *conflict*   ■ *conflict resolution.*

4 In pairs, write down as many different examples of conflict as you can, using the following headings:
   ■ *Local conflict*
   ■ *National conflict*
   ■ *International conflict.*

5 Read Figure Ⓐ carefully.
   (a) Who are the two main groups involved in the conflict at Parsons?
   (b) What are the causes of the conflict?
   (c) Which of the following ways of resolving the conflict do you think will be the most effective? Explain your answer.
   ■ *A strike by workers.*
   ■ *The management sack all 5,000 workers.*
   ■ *A Health and Safety Group is set up consisting of managers and workers.*
   ■ *The management and workers discuss their differences further.*
   ■ *The workers agree to a 10% pay increase in return for no jobs being lost.*

8.2 How did the conflict in Northern Ireland begin?

The next four pages look at one example of a national conflict. The conflict in Northern Ireland has existed for centuries. In the 20th and 21st centuries, governments have attempted to solve the conflict in several different ways.

Origins of the conflict

The conflict in Northern Ireland has a long history. Study Figure **A**, which traces the origins of the conflict.

Figure **A**

Northern Ireland conflict timeline

▼ William of Orange

JAMES·II

12th century	British settlers arrive in Ireland.
17th century	Protestants from Scotland and England take land from the native Irish Catholics. Irish Catholics rebel against British rule. The Protestant King William of Orange defeats Catholic King James II at the Battle of the Boyne in 1690.
19th century	Irish Parliament scrapped. Ireland becomes part of the United Kingdom.
20th century	Ireland is **partitioned** in 1923. Eire, consisting of 26 counties, is created in the South. Eire contains the majority of Ireland's Catholics. Northern Ireland is created in the North. Consisting of 6 counties, Northern Ireland's population has a majority of Protestants, though many Catholics also live in Northern Ireland.

20th-century conflict

From its creation in 1923, Northern Ireland was dominated by the Protestant majority. Catholics were discriminated against in jobs and housing and in politics. Many local councils were controlled by Protestants, and being a Catholic was a disadvantage in business.

In the late 1960s, many Catholics in Northern Ireland were involved in the Civil Rights Movement. This movement campaigned to get Catholics the same rights as Protestants. Violence erupted at some of the demonstrations, which led to the growth of a number of paramilitary or terrorist organisations.

From the early 1970s onwards, Northern Ireland's **terrorist** groups were in conflict with each other, and with the police and the army. Over 3,000 people have been killed as a result of the conflict in Northern Ireland since the late 1960s.

Terrorist groups in Northern Ireland

Northern Ireland's terrorist groups can be split into two main types: Republicans and Loyalists.

■ Republicans, also known as Nationalists, want to end Britain's rule in Northern Ireland. Many Catholics support Republican groups.

■ Loyalists, also known as Unionists, want Northern Ireland to remain part of the UK. Many Protestants support Loyalist groups.

There are several different Republican and Loyalist terrorist groups. Read the descriptions of two of the main terrorist groups set out in Figures **B** and **C**.

Figure B

The Irish Republican Army (IRA)

Founded in the 19th century, the IRA is responsible for the greatest number of killings in Northern Ireland. From the early 1970s the IRA carried out a violent campaign against the British army, police and ordinary civilians in Northern Ireland and on mainland Britain. The IRA has close links to a political party called Sinn Fein. Gerry Adams and Martin McGuinness are two of the leaders of Sinn Fein.

Figure C

The Ulster Defence Association (UDA)

The UDA is the largest Loyalist terrorist group in Northern Ireland. Set up in 1971, the UDA was formed to bring a number of different Protestant groups together. Closely linked to the UDA is the Ulster Freedom Fighters (UFF). Between them these two terrorist groups are responsible for the murder of a large number of Catholics in Northern Ireland.

SUMMARY

The origins of the Northern Ireland conflict can be traced back hundreds of years.

Since the 1970s there has been conflict in Northern Ireland.

This conflict has involved a number of groups. Republicans, or Nationalists, want Northern Ireland to be united with the rest of Ireland. Unionists, or Loyalists, want Britain to remain part of the United Kingdom.

ACTIVITIES

1   Study the timeline in Figure **A**.
    Then copy and match the century dates below with the correct key events.

Century	Key event
12th	■ Northern Ireland and Eire created. ■ The majority of Catholics live in Eire. ■ The majority of Protestants live in Northern Ireland.
17th	■ Ireland becomes part of the UK.
19th	■ Scottish and English Protestants take land from native Irish Catholics.
20th	■ The British arrive in Ireland.

2   Explain why the Civil Rights Movement developed in Northern Ireland in the 1960s.

3   Describe what each of the following two groups wants for Northern Ireland:
    ■ *Republicans*
    ■ *Loyalists.*

4   What methods have the IRA and the UDA used to achieve their aims?

5   Work in pairs. Write down ways that you think the conflict in Northern Ireland could be resolved.

8.3 How has conflict in Northern Ireland been resolved?

Since violence erupted in Northern Ireland in the 1970s there have been many attempts to end the conflict. Political parties in Northern Ireland, and the British, Irish and US Governments, have all played an important part in trying to reach a peaceful solution to the conflict.

Since 1985 there has been a peace process in place in Northern Ireland which has attempted to solve the conflict. The peace process has had many ups and downs. Study the timeline in Figure Ⓐ.

The Good Friday Agreement

In 1996 the IRA broke the **ceasefire** by bombing Canary Wharf in London. By this time Northern Ireland's political parties were discussing how to solve the conflict in a newly created Northern Ireland Assembly. Bill Clinton, the US President, encouraged the talks. Sinn Fein was kept out of the talks because of IRA violence.

▲ US President Bill Clinton meets the people of Omagh in September 1998.

Figure Ⓐ

The peace process timeline

1985	Britain and Eire (Republic of Ireland) sign the Anglo-Irish Agreement. Eire is to be consulted on matters relating to Northern Ireland.
1988–93	John Hume, Leader of the Social Democratic and Labour Party (SDLP), talks to Sinn Fein. Sinn Fein is encouraged to end its violence.
1993	The Downing Street Declaration is signed by the British and Eire Governments. Both governments call for an end to violence. Britain declares it has 'no selfish interest' in Northern Ireland.
1994	Loyalist terrorists and the IRA declare a ceasefire.

However, on Good Friday, 10 April 1998, all the major parties agreed to share power in Northern Ireland in a newly created Assembly. The Assembly was to be made up of 108 members who would all be elected by the people of Northern Ireland. The new Assembly would have the power to run Northern Ireland in areas such as housing, education and policing. Everyone in Northern Ireland was to have their human rights guaranteed and respected.

The people of Northern Ireland and Eire were asked to vote either *for* or *against* the Good Friday Agreement. In Northern Ireland 71% of the population voted for the Good Friday Agreement.

When the new Northern Ireland Assembly was created, David Trimble, leader of the Ulster Unionist Party, became First Minister. Martin McGuinness, a Sinn Fein leader, was made Minister for Education. Unionists and Nationalists were now sharing power together in Northern Ireland.

Problems with the peace process

Decommissioning

Unionist politicians demanded that all terrorists get rid of their weapons – this is called *decommissioning* and was a part of the Good Friday Agreement. The IRA have been slow to decommission their weapons. Outside helpers from South Africa and Finland have acted as observers when the terrorist groups have decommissioned their weapons.

Parades

Parades by the Protestant Orange Order have caused controversy. Many Catholics living where the parades take place want them banned. The issue of where Loyalist and Unionist groups are allowed to parade continues to be a problem.

Allegations of spying

In 2002 the Northern Ireland Assembly was suspended. This happened because the police arrested individuals accused of spying on the First Minister, David Trimble, on behalf of Sinn Fein. Unionist leaders felt they could no longer work together with Sinn Fein politicians. This was the biggest threat to the peace process so far.

▼ An Orange Parade at Drumcree in Northern Ireland.

SUMMARY

During the 1980s and 1990s a peace process developed in Northern Ireland.

The British and Irish Governments, the political parties of Northern Ireland and groups from abroad have all helped to stop the violence.

There are still problems. These are a threat to the peace process.

ACTIVITIES

1   What event happened in 1994 which stopped open violence in Northern Ireland?

2   Why was Sinn Fein kept out of the talks between Northern Ireland's political parties in 1996?

3   How have the following groups helped the peace process:
■   *the British and Irish Governments*
■   *political parties in Northern Ireland*
■   *the US Government*
■   *observers from abroad?*

4   Explain why the following issues continue to be a problem in Northern Ireland:
■   *decommissioning*
■   *parades*
■   *spying.*

5   'There was little support for the Good Friday Agreement in Northern Ireland.'
    A British newspaper reporter

Why can the reporter be accused of being selective in the use of facts?

8.4 How does the United Nations resolve conflicts?

The United Nations (UN)

The UN has an important role to play in resolving conflicts throughout the world. It was set up in 1945 after the end of the Second World War. In 1945, 50 countries signed the Charter of the United Nations. By 2002 the UN's membership had increased to 191 countries. When a country joins the UN it agrees to the UN Charter. The UN Charter has a number of aims. The three most important aims are:

- to promote human rights
- to stop and prevent wars from taking place
- to help less economically developed countries (LEDCs).

How is the UN organised?

With a budget of $2,535 billion in 2000–01, the UN employs thousands of people across the world. The General Assembly and the Security Council are two important parts of the UN.

The General Assembly

The General Assembly is made up of all member countries of the UN. The Assembly meets regularly to discuss any matters affecting its members. Each member of the UN has one vote in the General Assembly.

The Security Council

The Security Council is responsible for maintaining international peace and security. The Security Council has five permanent members:

- UK ■ USA ■ France ■ Russia ■ China.

As well as the five permanent members, the Security Council has ten non-permanent members who are elected every two years by the General Assembly.

Each of the five permanent members of the Security Council has the **power of veto**. This means that they can block decisions made by the Security Council if they do not like them. This gives more decision-making power to the five permanent members.

▼ A meeting of the UN Security Council.

How does the UN resolve conflicts?

In the last fifteen years there have been changes in the types of conflict around the world. More than 90% of conflicts now are within countries, rather than between countries. When two groups conflict violently with each other within a country, this is called a **civil war**.

Throughout the 1990s the UN was active in ending wars and maintaining peace in countries like the Democratic Republic of the Congo, Sierra Leone, El Salvador, Guatemala, Somalia and in the former Yugoslavia. The UN has helped to resolve some of these conflicts and to maintain peace in various ways.

- **Ceasefires and peace talks**

  The UN can call for a ceasefire during a conflict. This means that the two sides in conflict stop their fighting. The UN will then try to get opposing sides to talk with each other to stop and prevent a war.

- **Peace plans**

  In 1993 in the former Yugoslavia a civil war was taking place. The UN suggested a peace plan that would split the country amongst the three warring groups: the Serbs, Croats and Bosnian Muslims.

- **Peacekeeping**

  After a ceasefire the UN can send peacekeeping forces to a country to keep the two sides in a conflict apart. The UN's peacekeeping forces are made up of soldiers from UN member countries.

- **Sanctions**

  The UN uses sanctions to promote peace and security. **Trade sanctions** prevent countries from buying goods and selling them to other countries. **Arms embargoes** prevent the sale of weapons to some countries.

- **Military action**

  The UN can take military action to stop a conflict. This involves sending in troops and aircraft to stop wars.

▼ A UN peacekeeping patrol.

SUMMARY

The UN helps to promote peace and security throughout the world.

The General Assembly and the Security Council are two important parts of the UN.

The UN helps to resolve conflicts in a number of ways, e.g. by using peacekeeping forces.

ACTIVITIES

1 Describe the main aims of the UN.

2 Describe the role of:
   - *the General Assembly*
   - *the Security Council*
   in the UN.

3 Why do some countries on the Security Council have more power than others?

4 'The UN has little support from countries across the world. It has few members.'
   Provide evidence to show that this statement is exaggerated.

5 You are a newspaper reporter. You have been asked to write an article which describes the ways that the UN resolves conflicts. Your report should include:
   - *a newspaper name*
   - *a headline*
   - *background information describing the UN*
   - *a description of the various ways in which the UN settles conflicts.*

8.5 How does NATO resolve conflicts?

As well as the UN, the North Atlantic Treaty Organisation (NATO) is involved in helping to settle conflicts throughout the world.

What is NATO?

NATO was created in 1949. It was set up as an alliance between countries in Western Europe and North America. They agreed that if one member of NATO was attacked by another country, the NATO countries would help to defend them.

When NATO was created, countries in Western Europe and North America feared an attack by the Soviet Union (Russia) and her allies – a group of countries known as the **Warsaw Pact.**

Table **A** shows the original members of NATO when it was set up in 1949.

Table A

Original NATO members

- Belgium
- Canada
- Denmark
- France
- Iceland
- Italy
- Netherlands
- Norway
- Portugal
- United Kingdom
- United States

Since 1949 a number of other countries have joined NATO. For example, in 1952 Greece and Turkey joined, and in 1955 Germany became a member. Spain joined more recently, in 1982.

NATO enlargement

In the early 1990s the Warsaw Pact collapsed and the threat from Russia was not as great. Since then, many Eastern European countries have attempted to join NATO. Diagram **B** shows the new additions to NATO.

Why do countries want to join NATO?

There are two main reasons why countries want to join NATO:

- NATO provides security for countries. If one member of NATO is attacked, the other members will help them with military force.

- The economy of some countries has benefited because they have joined NATO. It is estimated that Hungary, the Czech Republic and Poland have seen a 50% increase in the number of foreign companies investing in these countries since they joined NATO.

Diagram B

The members of NATO in 2003

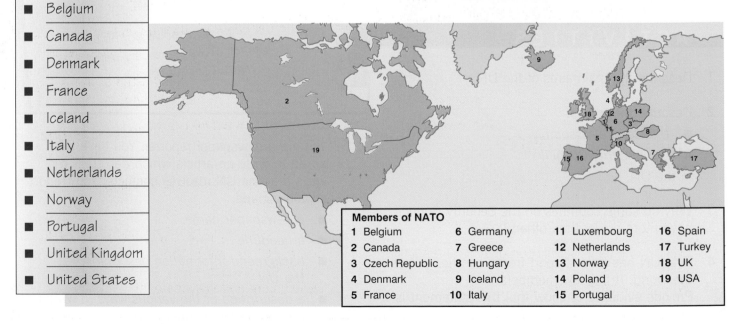

Members of NATO

1 Belgium	6 Germany	11 Luxembourg	16 Spain
2 Canada	7 Greece	12 Netherlands	17 Turkey
3 Czech Republic	8 Hungary	13 Norway	18 UK
4 Denmark	9 Iceland	14 Poland	19 USA
5 France	10 Italy	15 Portugal	

How is NATO organised?

The North Atlantic Council

The North Atlantic Council makes the major decisions affecting NATO. Representatives from each of NATO's member countries make up the North Atlantic Council. When major decisions are to be made, the heads of each government meet at a NATO Summit. For example, in November 2002, the heads of member countries met in the Czech capital of Prague to discuss the issue of NATO enlargement.

One of the other issues agreed upon in Prague was the setting up of a **rapid reaction force** of 20,000 troops from NATO members, which could be sent anywhere in the world. The lack of such a force, which could be put into war quickly, was one of the reasons why NATO was not heavily involved in the US attack on Afghanistan in 2001. One of the jobs of the rapid reaction force would be to fight terrorism.

The Secretary General

The spokesperson for NATO is called the Secretary General. In 1999, Lord Robertson, a Scot, became NATO's Secretary General.

How does NATO resolve conflicts?

NATO helps to settle conflicts in much the same way as the UN does (see pages 114–115 and Diagram **C** below).

The future of NATO

With the collapse of the Warsaw Pact, many people question whether or not NATO has a future to play in world affairs. It has received both good and bad reports from the press. For example, in 1999, NATO launched an 11-week campaign of air strikes against Yugoslavia. It did this to try to stop conflict between the government of Yugoslavia and the people of Kosovo. However, NATO's bombing campaigns killed many innocent civilians.

Some people are also concerned about the role of the USA in NATO. Critics say that the USA has too much influence over what NATO does.

However, many people see a continuing role for NATO in international crises and hope that it will remain a strong force in the future.

Diagram C

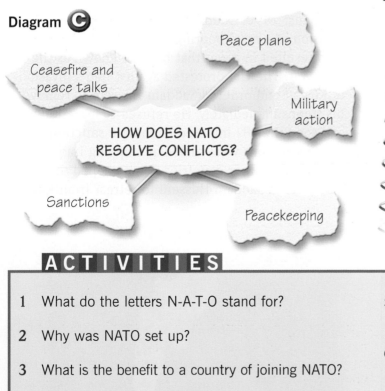

Peace plans

Ceasefire and peace talks

Military action

HOW DOES NATO RESOLVE CONFLICTS?

Sanctions

Peacekeeping

SUMMARY

NATO was set up in 1949.

Since 1949 NATO has grown in size. More countries have joined the organisation.

NATO helps to settle disputes in much the same way as the UN.

NATO is headed by the Secretary General.

ACTIVITIES

1 What do the letters N-A-T-O stand for?

2 Why was NATO set up?

3 What is the benefit to a country of joining NATO?

4 Who is the head of NATO?

5 What criticisms have been made of NATO in recent years?

6 You can discover more about the work of NATO and the UN in international conflicts. To do this, visit their websites at:
www.un.org and www.nato.int

8.6 What was the Gulf War?

Iraq is a country that is situated in the Gulf region of the Middle East (Diagram **A**). It has seen a great deal of conflict in recent years. Its problems are linked to the country's leader – Saddam Hussein. The UN and NATO have both been involved in this conflict and in attempts to resolve it.

Who is Saddam Hussein?

The timeline in Figure **B** highlights some of the main events concerning Saddam Hussein.

Diagram **B**

Diagram **A**   Iraq in the Middle East

▲ Saddam Hussein

- Saddam Hussein was born in 1937 in Iraq.

- In 1956 he joined the Arab Baath Socialist Party.

- In 1959 Hussein participated in an assassination attempt on the Iraqi Prime Minister.

- In 1968 he participated in an armed revolt, which led to the Baath Party taking power in Iraq.

- In 1979 Hussein became the new president of Iraq, killing large numbers of his rivals in the process.

- From 1979 there were numerous reported cases of torture and unlawful killings in Iraq. Saddam Hussein suspended free elections.

- Saddam Hussein was defeated by coalition Forces in 2003.

The Gulf War

In August 1990, Suddam Hussein ordered the invasion of a neighbouring country called Kuwait. This resulted in a war that became known as the Gulf War. The UN protested against Iraq's invasion of Kuwait and ordered Saddam Hussein to remove his troops immediately. He refused to leave Kuwait and soon the UN imposed **economic sanctions**. These sanctions were aimed at stopping Iraq from trading with other countries. It was hoped this would force Saddam Hussein to retreat from Kuwait.

However, Iraq did not leave Kuwait. The UN, NATO and troops from countries across the world were involved in the war to force Iraq to leave Kuwait. It became known as Operation Desert Storm.

Countries in the West were very worried by what Iraq had done. By taking control of Kuwait, Saddam Hussein had invaded another nation. It also meant he would have control of a large proportion of the world's oil. Oil is a very powerful commodity in world trade and it was feared that Saddam would use this power in a damaging way.

Many countries saw the Gulf War as a way of actually making the world less dangerous. The US President said:

> What is at stake is more than one small country, it is a big idea – a new world order, where diverse nations are drawn together in a common cause to achieve the universal aspirations of mankind: peace and security, freedom and the rule of law.
>
> *President George Bush, 1991*

For this reason, many countries across the world were involved in fighting against Iraq, with the USA taking the lead. The fighting lasted five weeks and finally ended in February 1991.

▼ US President George Bush

What was agreed?

Iraq lost the war on 6 April 1991, and agreed to a permanent ceasefire. One of the terms of the ceasefire was that Iraq should show the UN its chemical and biological weapons, and get rid of its most dangerous weapons and bombs. Saddam Hussein was very unwilling to co-operate with these demands. This resulted in the UN continuing its policy of imposing economic sanctions against Iraq.

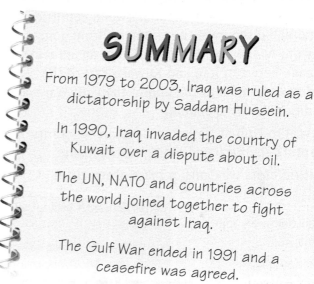

SUMMARY

From 1979 to 2003, Iraq was ruled as a dictatorship by Saddam Hussein.

In 1990, Iraq invaded the country of Kuwait over a dispute about oil.

The UN, NATO and countries across the world joined together to fight against Iraq.

The Gulf War ended in 1991 and a ceasefire was agreed.

ACTIVITIES

1 When did Saddam Hussein invade Kuwait?

2 What two steps did the UN take because of this invasion?

3 Can you suggest why countries in the West were very worried when Iraq invaded Kuwait?

4 What terms were agreed at the ceasefire?

5 'Iraq is not a dictatorship. Saddam Hussein got 100% of the votes in the last election.' Do you agree with this statement? Explain your answer.

6 You might like to find out more about the Gulf War. You can visit a website such as:
www.news.bbc.co.uk
You could also carry out a search by entering 'Gulf War' or 'Saddam Hussein'.

8.7 Why was Iraq involved in weapons inspections?

The peace agreement

When conflicts end, part of the peacekeeping process involves writing a peace agreement. The United Nations is often involved in this and makes sure that any agreement made between countries is fair and will discourage the countries from going to war again. At the end of the Gulf War, an agreement was made between Iraq and Kuwait. Part of the ceasefire agreement at the end of the Gulf War was a condition that Iraq should:

- reveal to United Nations inspectors where it kept its chemical and biological weapons
- get rid of its weapons of mass destruction.

▼ A soldier in an anti-chemical suit.

> **Chemical and biological weapons**
>
> These weapons are gases that lead to a very painful death if they are simply breathed in or touch a person's skin. Napalm and anthrax are two examples of such weapons.

Weapons inspections

The members of the UN were very unhappy that these weapons might be in the hands of a state like Iraq, which had acted in a dangerous way before.

In April 1991, the UN set up a group to monitor the situation. It wanted to make sure that Saddam Hussein kept his part of the agreement.

This group was called UNIKOM (United Nations Iraq-Kuwait Observer Mission). It would carefully check the borders between Iraq and Kuwait (in case of another invasion) and check on Iraq's decommissioning of weapons.

▼ A UN inspector in Baghdad.

> **Weapons of mass destruction**
>
> These weapons usually come in the form of nuclear weapons and can kill millions of people instantly. They are usually loaded into missiles that can reach targets up to several thousand miles away.

Problems with weapons inspections

At first, weapons and the factories in which they were produced were destroyed and dismantled. Inspectors found weapons that the Iraqis had tried to hide and factories that they had denied ever having.

However, Iraq very soon became unwilling to co-operate with the weapons inspectors and they found their job very difficult.

In the late 1990s, the UN inspectors left the country, claiming that Iraqi officials were obstructing their work. This resulted in much disagreement between the UN and Iraq. Saddam Hussein's failure to allow weapons inspectors into his country further weakened relations between Iraq and the USA and UK.

Renewed weapons inspections

In November 2002, the inspections began again. The inspection group was now called UNMOVIC. UN weapons inspectors insisted that Iraq must provide a list of any chemical or biological weapons that it had. They also visited factories that they suspected might be making weapons. This included mosques and presidential palaces – places the weapons inspectors had not been able to examine in the 1990s. The UN agreed that there would be very serious consequences for Saddam Hussein's regime if the inspectors were not allowed to look where they wanted to.

▼ United Nations troops on the move.

War on Iraq – 2003

In early 2003 a decision was made by coalition countries, led by the USA and UK, that an invasion of Iraq should take place as a result of Saddam Hussein's refusal to co-operate with the weapons inspectors. This was a controversial move, as the United Nations failed to approve the decision. However, coalition forces defeated Saddam's Iraqi troops and invaded the capital, Baghdad, in April 2003. The future of Iraq is still uncertain.

SUMMARY

The UN is often involved in making peace agreements when wars end.

At the end of the Gulf War, the UN ordered Iraq to reveal the extent of its biological and chemical weapons and weapons of mass destruction.

Iraq made it difficult for the UN to check its stock of weapons.

In November 2002, weapons inspectors revisited Iraq.

ACTIVITIES

1   Why are peace agreements signed at the end of wars?

2   Name two important features of the peace agreement signed at the end of the Gulf War.

3   Describe what is meant by:
   ■ *chemical and biological weapons*
   ■ *weapons of mass destruction.*

4   'Why is the UN demanding that we get rid of these weapons? They are of no harm to anyone.'   *Iraqi politician*
   Why was the UN keen for Iraq to get rid of its chemical and biological weapons and any weapons of mass destruction?

5   Write a report on the results of the UN weapons inspections that began in Iraq in 2002. Has the UN managed to keep the peace in the Gulf?

8.8 How do we combat terrorism?

What is terrorism?

Terrorism occurs when extreme action is taken by a group to publicise their cause. It often involves the loss of life and events that attract a great deal of attention from the media.

What happened in the USA on 11 September 2001?

On 11 September 2001 at 8.58 am, the Twin Towers of the World Trade Center in New York were destroyed by two aeroplanes crashing into them. At first people thought it had been a terrible accident. However, very soon they realised that this was the work of terrorists. The world was shocked. Horrific pictures were transmitted on television screens which stunned people all over the globe. The media had a big impact on how people reacted to the disaster.

▲ Osama bin Laden

Who was to blame?

At the top of the list of terrorist suspects was Osama bin Laden, leader of the Al Qaeda group of Islamic terrorists. His organisation was blamed for the horrible events of 11 September, and the USA declared a 'War on Terror'.

The UN and NATO became involved in the dispute and very soon other countries began to involve themselves too. The events of 11 September were seen as an attack on democracy across the world, and not just in the USA.

How was the conflict resolved?

Osama bin Laden was known to be in a country called Afghanistan. As part of the 'War on Terror', the USA wanted Afghanistan to hand over bin Laden, but the ruling Taliban authorities there decided simply to ask him to leave voluntarily. American forces and their allies went to war with the Taliban. In November 2001 the Taliban forces retreated. but Osama bin Laden was not captured.

Despite the USA's 'War on Terror', bin Laden proved very difficult for the UN and NATO forces to trace. The Al Qaeda terrorist organisation has been linked to many attacks across the world since 11 September. One of the most serious took place on the Indonesian island of Bali where, on 12 October 2002, a huge bomb exploded outside a nightclub packed with people in the seaside resort of Kuta Beach. A total of 180 holidaymakers were killed.

▼ The terrorist attack on New York, 11 September 2001.

No one admitted to carrying out the attack but very soon Osama bin Laden's Al Qaeda group was blamed. The US President, George Bush, announced to the world that, once again, Al Qaeda would be a top priority in his country's fight against terrorism.

The attack on Bali was very worrying for countries in the West. Although the fighting in Afghanistan was now over, it was clear that the Al Qaeda network was still very strong and capable of carrying out more attacks. The danger with terrorists is that countries never know where or when they will strike next. Such conflicts prove very difficult for countries to resolve.

The role of the media

The media played a major role in broadcasting all of these events. Television and newspapers are very powerful and the images they send out across the world can often affect people's opinions of events. They used 'shock tactics' when they showed live images of the Twin Towers, and newspapers were full of pictures showing the destroyed Bali nightclub.

The war in Afghanistan was also given a lot of coverage, although the military did not allow cameras access to everything. For example, the Western media did not show many pictures of civilians who were killed by US bombs. This is because public support is needed to enable democratic governments to carry out such military campaigns.

Terrorism remains a major area of conflict in our society and around the world. It is a difficult conflict to resolve, and will certainly be a major issue in our global society for many years (Figure Ⓐ).

Figure Ⓐ

No one has any doubts that the war against Al Qaeda and its offshoots will last for many years. It has become truly international and the terrorists have given notice that they will target vulnerable Westerners wherever they can – throughout the world.

Panorama broadcast on BBC1, 20 October 2002

▼ Taliban gunmen show off their weapons to foreign journalists in Afghanistan.

SUMMARY

Terrorist organisations work from different countries across the world.

The 'War on Terror' involves many nations.

The Al Qaeda group have been blamed for many acts of terrorism.

The media plays a major role in broadcasting the events.

Combating terrorism across the world is very difficult.

ACTIVITIES

1 What is meant by *terrorism*?

2 Describe the events that took place on 11 September 2001 in New York.

3 Who was blamed for this attack?

4 How was the conflict resolved?

5 Why was the attack on Bali in October 2002 of particular concern to countries in the West?

6 Look carefully at Figure Ⓐ.
'Television broadcasters are always biased in their reporting of international events.'
What arguments can be made for and against this statement?

7 You might like to find out more about these events and subjects. Visit a website such as: www.news.bbc.co.uk

Glossary

A

Additional Member System (AMS) A type of electoral system.

Arms embargo Prevention of the sale of weapons to some countries.

Asylum-seeker A person who flees their own country.

B

Back benches Where the majority of MPs sit in the House of Commons.

Bias Leaning in favour of one viewpoint.

Bilateral aid When aid is given from one country to another country.

Bill An idea for a new law.

Broadsheet Newspaper that reports issues in depth.

C

Cabinet Body of people who make up the top ministers in government.

Ceasefire Agreement between two countries to suspend fighting.

Children's Hearing System Deals with children in Scotland who break the law or are in danger.

Citizenship When people take an active part in society.

Civil court Concerned with solving disputes between individuals.

Civil war War between two sides in the same country.

Clear-up rate Percentage of crimes reported to the police that are solved.

Coalition When two or more groups join together, usually parties in a government.

Committee Group of MPs who discuss new laws and suggest changes to them.

Community Usually people who live in the same area.

Concession When people make allowances in order to come to an agreement.

Conflict Disagreement between two or more people or groups.

Constituency Area which elects an MP to represent that area in Parliament.

Constituent Someone who has a right to vote for the representative of their electoral area (constituency).

Constitution Statement of the rights of citizens in a democracy.

Corporal punishment The use of force to control children.

Criminal court Concerned with crimes against the community, e.g. murder.

Criminal responsibility The age at which individuals can be held responsible for committing crimes.

D

Debate Name given to the process when MPs discuss important issues.

Debt Money that is borrowed but cannot be repaid.

Democracy Government where citizens in a country have rights and responsibilities.

Despatch box Ceremonial box used in Parliament.

Devolution When power is transferred from one Parliament to another.

Dictatorship Leadership by one ruler, where citizens have no rights and responsibilities.

Direct democracy System where citizens are directly involved in making laws.

Discrimination Denial of equal opportunities, usually on the basis of race or religion.

District Court Deals with minor crimes in Scotland.

E

Economic sanction Prevents a particular country from buying and selling goods to other countries.

Economics Deals with the study of the economy.

Economy Allows people to buy and sell goods and services.

Election When citizens cast a vote.

Electoral register List of people who can vote in a constituency.

Enlargement Process of making the European Union larger.

Entrepreneur Person who makes money from his or her own ideas.

Euro Name given to the currency of the European Union.

European Union (EU) Countries in Europe that are bound together by certain agreements. It was originally known as the European Economic Community (EEC).

Exaggeration When facts are distorted in some way.

F

Front benches Where Ministers and leading members of the opposition sit in the House of Commons.

G

Global society Reliance by countries across the world on each other, e.g. by trade.

Globalisation When countries across the world rely on each other.

Government Name given to the group of people who run a country.

Government Minister MP who is in charge of a government department or part of one.

H

High Court of the Justiciary Scottish court that tries serious crimes such as robbery and murder.

House of Commons Elected part of the UK Parliament.

House of Lords Unelected part of the UK Parliament.

Human rights Rights that every human being should be entitled to.

Humanitarian aid Aid that is given to help people, usually after a disaster.

I

Identity Individual characteristics by which a person or group is easily recognised.

Immigration Movement of people from one country into another country.

Income tax Tax paid to the government as a percentage of a person's wage.

Independence Scotland breaking away from the rest of the UK.

Internet Provides access via a computer to information from across the world.

J

Justice of the Peace Person who controls and decides upon the guilt of the accused in District Courts.

L

Law A standard that the government enforces through the police.

Left wing Belief in equality and the use of government to achieve it.

Legal right Something that people can claim by law, e.g. to vote at age 18 in the UK.

Less economically developed country (LEDC) Country with an economy that does not create much wealth.

List MSPs Members of the Scottish Parliament elected from the list.

Living standards The conditions under which people live.

Lobbying Occurs when a person or group tries to influence an MP.

M

Mace Ornate pole which is a symbol of the House of Commons.

Majority When one party has the most seats in the House of Commons.

Manifesto Statement of a political party's policies.

Media Name for means of communication, e.g. radio, TV, internet.

Member of Parliament (MP) Representative elected to the House of Commons.

Member of the European Parliament (MEP) Elected representative of the European Parliament.

Member of the Scottish Parliament (MSP) Representative elected to the Scottish Parliament.

Monarch Head of state in a country, e.g. king or queen.

More economically developed country (MEDC) Country with an economy that creates a great deal of wealth.

Multicultural society A society made up of many different races.

Multinational company/corporation Company that conducts business in more the one country.

N

National minimum wage Lowest hourly rate that companies can legally pay their employees.

Needs Basic requirements of all people.

Non-governmental organisation (NGO) Organisation that attempts to help meet a country's needs.

O

Offence Less serious criminal act than a crime, e.g. speeding.

Opposition All the political parties that are not in government.

P

Parliament Place where laws are made in Britain.

Participation When people take part in society.

Partition A separation.

Persecution Making individuals or groups suffer because of negative views held about them.

Political party Group of people with the same political beliefs.

Positive discrimination Promoting certain groups above others to achieve fairness.

Poverty When people cannot afford their basic needs.

Power of veto Saying 'no': allows an organisation or country to overturn a situation.

Prejudice When people hold negative views that are not based on fact.

Press Code List of rules which the press should adhere to.

Press Complaints Commission Body that addresses complaints against the press.

Pressure group Group that puts pressure on organisations to make changes.

Prime Minister Leader of the government.

Prime Minister's Question Time When a Prime Minister is questioned by other MPs. Takes place once a week in the House of Commons.

Private bill Bill presented to the House of Commons by an MP.

Procurator Fiscal Carries out the prosecution of accused people in Scottish courts.

Producer Company or country that make goods.

Public Private Partnership (PPP) Public and private companies co-operating together, e.g. to build a new school.

Q

Question Time When a government Minister is questioned by other MPs.

R

Racial stereotype Inaccurate information about racial groups, e.g. 'the Scots are red-haired and knobbly-kneed'.

Racism Discrimination on the basis of race.

Rapid reaction force Troops from NATO member countries which are sent into conflict situations.

Referendum When people are asked their opinion on a political issue.

Reported crime Crime that has taken place and is reported to the police.

Reporter Person who decides if a child in Scotland should be referred to the Children's Hearing System.

Representative democracy System where representatives make laws on behalf of citizens.

Responsibilities When people act in the correct manner to protect their rights.

Right wing Belief in a small amount of government interference.

Rights Those areas to which, as members of society, we are entitled.

Royal Assent When the Queen signs a new law.

Rule A standard that individuals are expected to follow.

S

Shadow Cabinet Leading politicians who make policies for the largest opposition party.

Sheriff Court The second highest court in Scotland.

Single market A common trading system between members of the European Union.

Social Chapter Agreement between European Union members on social conditions.

Society Group of people who share the same characteristics.

Speaker The individual who controls proceedings in the House of Commons.

Stereotype Impression made by someone based on an incomplete mental picture.

Suffragettes Group of women who campaigned for the right of women in Britain to vote.

Summary cases Cases in the Sheriff Court where a judge, and not a jury, decides upon guilt.

Survey A list of questions people are asked in order to find out their views on particular issues.

T

Tabloid Newspaper that reports issues in basic detail.

Terrorist Member of a group that takes extreme action to publicise its cause.

Tied aid Aid given to a country that has to be spent on things provided by the donor nation.

Trade sanctions When a country or countries refuse to trade with another country.

U

Unionist Name given to those who favour the United Kingdom.

United Nations (UN) Organisation comprising the majority of the world's nations.

United Nations Convention on the Rights of the Child (CRC) List of rights which the UN says that every child should have.

United Nations Universal Declaration of Human Rights (UDHR) List of rights which the UN says that every human should have.

Unreported crime Crime that has taken place but is not reported to the police.

W

Warsaw Pact Alliance of Eastern European countries during the Cold War period.

Acknowledgements

The authors and publishers would like to thank the following for permission to reproduce copyright photographs and images in this book:

Comic Relief: 102 (both); Corel 461 (NT): 26, 107, 116; Corel 587 (NT): 75; Empics: 10 (top); Eye Ubiquitous: 92, 106; Hulton Archive: 15, 29, 110 (both); L&B Police: 17, 22 (both); Mary Evans Picture Library: v, 67; PA Photos: 28, 43, 49, 50, 83; PA Photos/Neil Munns: 45; PA Photos/Stefan Rousseau: 66; PA Photos/David Cheskin: 71; PA Photos/Ben Curtis: 74, PA Photos/Owen Humphries: 88; PA Photos/ David Kendall: 89; PA Photos/EPA: 91, 108, 120 (right); Popperfoto/Reuters/Dan Chung: 90, 111; Popperfoto/ Reuters/Paul McErlane: 113 (left); Rex Features: 12, 27, 30 (bottom), 32 (both), 46, 47, 48, 51, 54, 65, 77, 79, 81, 87, 94, 99, 101, 104 (right), 113 (right), 115, 118 (both), 119 (both), 120 (left), 121, 122 (both); Rex Features/Sipa: 104 (left), 114; Rex Features/PBA: 107; 112; Save the Children: 103; Scotland in Focus: 97; Scotsman Publications: 16, 19, 30 (top), 36, 40, 53, 72; Shout Picture Library: 86; Still Moving Pictures: 60, 63; Trip/Eye Ubiquitous: 100; Yiorgos Nikiteas: 8, 10 (bottom), 23, 84.

Cover and title page images: Scottish Parliamentary Corporate Body/RMJM (background image); (inset images, left to right) Scottish Parliamentary Corporate Body/RMJM, David Hoffman Photo Library, PA Photos, L. Brennan/Associated Press, EWI/Creativ Collection (NT), SW Productions/Photodisc/Getty.

Thanks are also due to the following for permission to reproduce text items:

BBC World Service: 32; *Scotland on Sunday*: 23; Newsquest (Herald and Evening Times) Ltd: 31; Amnesty International: 34; Comic Relief: 102; Save the Children: 103.

Every effort has been made to trace copyright holders. The publishers apologise to anyone whose rights have been inadvertently overlooked, and will be happy to rectify any errors or omissions at the earliest opportunity.